M. P. Robinson

AMX-30
Char de Bataille
1966–2006
vol. II

*This book is dedicated
to Noel Legros
and Guy Gibeau.*

Introduction

This second volume of *AMX-30 Char de Bataille* concludes the study of the 47 year career of the AMX-30 battle tank in French service. It describes the service life and modernization of the AMX-30 design in the early 1980s and again in the mid 1990s. In the same period the French Army's divisional structure changed considerably, as did the organization of the *regiment blindée* from 1984 onwards. After the Cold War ended in 1989-1990, the AMX-30B slowly disappeared from the order of battle of the French Army, although the AMX-30B2 saw combat in the 1991 liberation of Kuwait. Delays to production of the Leclerc MBT resulted in the retention of the AMX-30B2 in service as a gun tank until 2006, and as a training vehicle to this day. Photographic coverage in this volume is focused on the AMX-30B2, and includes archival and private photos of the technical milestones that have marked a remarkably long career.

The Author would like to thank the following people

I thank Tomasz Basarabowicz for his help with organizing this project with Kagero. I would like to express my sincere gratitude to Pierre Delattre, Olivier Carneau, and Claude Balmefrezol who encouraged my research and ensured I was put in touch with some of France's experts on the AMX-30 series. My gratitude to Thomas Seignon, Christophe Legrand, Noel Legros, and Jacques Maillard for their contribution to this volume cannot be stated enough. I thank Steven Zaloga, Julie Ludmann, Guy Gibeau, Christian Guibelin, David Rotaris, Luis Pitarch Carrion, Triantafyllos Metsovitis, Francis Cany, Jonathan Cany, Philippe Besson, Marcel Toulon, Stelios Markides, Paul Baron, Zurich, Christian Berg and Lionel Gonnet for their contribution of research material, photographs and encouragement. The author would also like to salute the efforts of Xavier Lena, Jean-Francois Brilliant, Pierre Piveteau, Michel Loyauté, Claude Aicardi, Henri Azema and the many other French armoured enthusiasts and historians who have made researching this work possible by maintaining websites that have enabled discussion and study of these vehicles and the army they served. Lastly, I must thank my wife Nisa and our children Leif, Owyn, Alexandria, Griffin and Thor for their patience in preparing this second volume.

M.P. Robinson

AMX-30. Char de Bataille 1966–2006. Vol. II • M.P. Robinson • First edition • LUBLIN 2014

© All English Language Rights Reserved. With the exception of quoting brief passages for the purposes of review, no part of this publication may be reproduced without prior written permission from the Publisher. Nazwa serii zastrzeżona w UP RP • ISBN 978-83-64596-04-9

Editors: M.P. Robinson, Tomasz Basarabowicz • Color profiles: Sławomir Zajączkowski
• Design: KAGERO STUDIO, Marcin Wachowicz

Oficyna Wydawnicza KAGERO
Akacjowa 100, Turka, os. Borek, 20-258 Lublin 62, Poland, phone/fax: (+48) 81 501 21 05
www.kagero.pl • e-mail: kagero@kagero.pl, marketing@kagero.pl
w w w . k a g e r o . p l

The AMX-30B in service in the 1970s: a proven design well received by the *Arme Blindée Cavalerie* from November 1966 onwards. Technology was fast evolving in the 1970s however and the AMX-30B changed little during the decade. Over twenty French armoured regiments were equipped with the AMX-30B by 1981. [Jacques Maillard]

The AMX-30 Crew

The AMX-30B's crew consisted of four men, and it followed a conventional layout with the driver at the front left, the fighting compartment in the center of the tank and the engine and transmission at the rear of the vehicle. Most of the men in the *Arme Blindée Cavalerie* (or ABC as it was usually abbreviated to) were *appelés*; or conscripts. In the early days, armoured regiments differed in how they approached how to deploy their professional and conscript soldiers with the new tank.

Some regiments only employed professional soldiers as tank commanders and NCOs in their armoured squadrons and employed conscript gunners and loaders. Conscripts selected for promotion in these cases could more often be found in the *escadron porté* or the *escadron de commandement*. Conscript junior officers and non-commissioned officers eventually became more common in the armoured squadrons as time passed. In the early days of the AMX-30's service some regiments only used regular soldiers (*engagés*) for crew commanders and as drivers. The first escadron to get the new tanks in a regiment

A real weakness of the AMX-30B power train was the 5-SD-200D transmission of the original design, which was never as reliable as the army would have expected it to be. This vehicle of the *6e Régiment de Dragons* has suffered a transmission failure on the Baumholder training ground in 1979. The crew commander on the left looks frustrated, whilst the mechanic to his right looks positively thrilled at the prospect of a pack lift. Transmission failure was a recurrent problem that was partly solved by better quality components, but the real solution was the Minerva transmission introduced on the AMX-30B2. [Claude Balmefrezol]

A *6e Régiment de Dragons* AMX-30B broken down on the training ground in the late 1970s. This photo was taken by an AMX-30D recovery vehicle crewman from the *Atelier Regimentaire*. [Christian Guibelin]

was a matter of the regimental commander's choice. The *5e Regiment de Cuirassiers* received sufficient AMX-30B in the spring of 1969 to re-equip an *escadron* previously serving on AMX-13 SS11 light tanks. By the latter years of the AMX-30B's service in some regiments only the senior non-commissioned officers and officers in an armoured regiment were professional soldiers. This came about as a result of the creation of a specialised conscript category in 1975 to provide a regular supply of specialised personnel in key roles. The new category was entitled *engagé volontaire spécialiste*, with driver or gunner specialization. The new category was embraced to varying degrees within the regiments of the ABC.

All crew received two months of basic training known as *Formation Élementaire Toutes Armes (FETTA)*, after which drivers were sent to the (CIABC = *Centre d'Instruction de l'Arme Blindée Cavalerie*), near Marseille at Carpiagne for specialisation training. Gunners received their gunnery courses at the *Corps de Troupes* level (with their regiments), or at Carpiagne with further training conducted within their regiments. The loader-operator (*radio-chargeur* or *Romeo Charlie* in French) followed a similar path, with much of the training being conducted in the regimental training cadre or *escadron d'instruction*, which was tasked with streaming suitably trained young conscripts into the *escadrons* for inclusion into the tank crews. Each *peloton* was commanded by a *sous-lieutenant* or a *lieutenant* but this too was subject to some variation, depending on the regiment. A senior non-commissioned officer, or a junior officer, would serve as a second in command known as a *sous-officier adjoint* (or SOA). The ideal norm expected to be established was to eventually use conscripts for all crew positions, although the reality of crewing the tanks always differed between the various regiments of the ABC.

As in any tank, the AMX-30B commander had to conduct engagements, maintain communication with the rest of the *peloton* and be responsible for his tank and the lives of his crew. The TOP-7 cupola gave the commander a panoramic view, and it incorporated a binocular M267 sight as well as ten M248 observation periscopes. With operations at night being accorded great importance, the commander would swap the binocular M267 sight for an infra-red OB23A sight. The TOP-7 could contra-rotate and the commander could line up the main armament on any target he observed. Asides from his cupola machine gun, after the introduction of the fully automatic 20mm CN20 F2 co-axial armament in the mid-1970s, the commander was expected to conduct any anti-aircraft engagements from his cupola due to its panoramic view. The main design purpose of this weapon on the AMX-30 series was as an anti-helicopter weapon system, but otherwise it was usually employed in the same manner as the 12.7mm co-axial weapon had been. With the ability to penetrate 15mm of armour at 1000 meters with armour piercing ammunition, or to fire high explosive rounds, it would have served admirably as a weapon against armoured personnel carriers or against infantry.

The later style of crew uniform worn from the mid 1980s onwards. These AMX-30Bs are from the *2e Escadron*, 501e RCC, France's only completely professional escadron in the *Arme Blindée Cavalerie* during the 1980s. [D. Rotaris]

Another AMX-30B undergoing a pack lift accompanied by a Berliet wrecker and an AMX-30D in the early 1980s. The AMX-30B2 enjoyed a much better mechanical reputation because of the improvement in transmission reliability. [Thomas Seignon]

The AMX-30B's entrance into service took place in spite of the original transmission's obvious weakness and complexity, and the first armoured regiments equipping with the new tank addressed this by using experienced drivers. The *1e Régiment de Cuirassiers* took a draft of fifty four *engagés* from Carpiagne as drivers in 1969 when the new AMX-30Bs arrived. Once the new tanks were in service the conscript drivers gradually took over. The AMX-30B was driven with two levers much like the wartime tanks, a step backwards from the relatively luxurious driving arrangements in the M47 Patton. The AMX-30B's driver had the hard task of mastering manual gear changes, and the various drivers' drills required to minimise wear on the transmission. The 5-SD-200D transmission incorporated five forward speeds and five reverse speeds and required close attention to the engine RPMs for gear changes. Driving the AMX-30B was still easier than the AMX-13, which had an even more demand-

The DX150 fire training system produced by GIRAVION DORAND (today GDI) which permitted the commander and gunner to train in the tank in any open area of a training ground. The system incorporated a target in the gunner's sight whose range had to be estimated by the commander, who would then initiate a simulated firing drill. As we can see by the NATO marking on the mudguard, the tank is a *6e Régiment de Cuirassiers* AMX-30B. [Marcel Toulon]

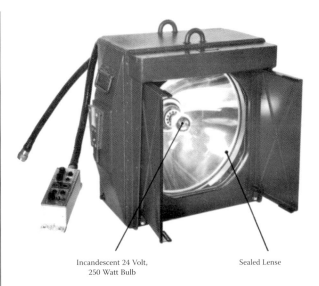

Incandescent 24 Volt,
250 Watt Bulb

Sealed Lense

PH-8B Searchlight, Shutters Open, White Light Mode

The PH-8B infrared and white light searchlight. By the early 1980s the AMX-30B's reliance on infrared systems for nocturnal combat was also considered a liability, although the PH-8B endured into the 1990s even after the AMX-30B was withdrawn and was fitted as standard on the AMX-30B2, although only as a white light system. [Thomas Seignon]

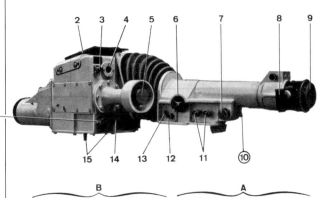

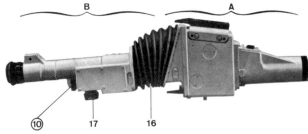

A – Oscilating Section
B – Fixed Section

1 – Inclination Level Light	10 – Colour screen switch
2 – Attachment Bracket	11 – Micrometer Rheostat (trunnion tilt)
3 – Power Socket for Sight Illumination	12 – Fuse
4 – Level Control	13 – Override
5 – Deviation Control Button	14 – Illumination Bulb (micrometer)
6 – Symbology Diaphragm Control	15 – Locator Guide Rails
7 – Spares box (bulbs, fuses)	16 – Bellows
8 – Telescope Adjustment Knob	17 – Range Micrometer Adjustment Button
9 – Eyepiece	

The M271 gunner's sight and the OB17A infra red sight were cutting edge technology in the mid 1960s, but by the late 1970s, these systems were reliable if dated technology. The COTAC's M581.03A and DIVT-13 combination that were adopted in the AMX-30B2 gave the gunner a far superior fire control system. [Thomas Seignon]

1. PH-9A searchlight
2. OB-23A Binocular sight fitted to M270 Periscopic Sight
3. OB-17A Night Vision Periscope.

The commander and gunner both employed infrared swap sights on the AMX-30B, which would be changed for the day sights as required. The problem with the use of infrared light as a night fighting system by 1980 was the ease with which it could be detected by newer sensor equipment developed in the late 1970s. [Thomas Seignon]

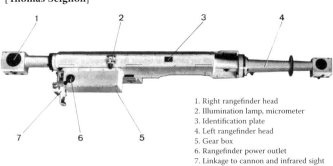

1. Right rangefinder head
2. Illumination lamp, micrometer
3. Identification plate
4. Left rangefinder head
5. Gear box
6. Rangefinder power outlet
7. Linkage to cannon and infrared sight

Rangefinder, Sight M208 (seen from front)

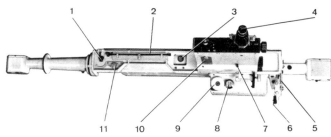

1. Image azimuth adjustment
2. Image adjustment lever
3. Range scale illumination lamp
4. Eyepiece
5. Immobilisation plate for transporting rangefinder dismounted
6. Image adjustment screw for enlargement
7. Diaphragm
8. Ballistic correction button
9. Sillicagel chamber, rangefinder body
10. Spares box (fuses, bulbs, sillicagel)
11. Eyepiece key

Rangefinder, Sight M208 (seen from rear)

The M208 turret coincidence rangefinder was a critical component of the AMX-30B and French faith in this type of fire control system had arisen from the M47's long service in the *Arme Blindée Cavalerie*. While the CN 105 F1 and M208 had enjoyed excellent target acquisition and accuracy for its day firing OCC ammunition in the 1960s and 1970s, the era of the laser rangefinder brought gunnery to a higher level of technology. [Thomas Seignon]

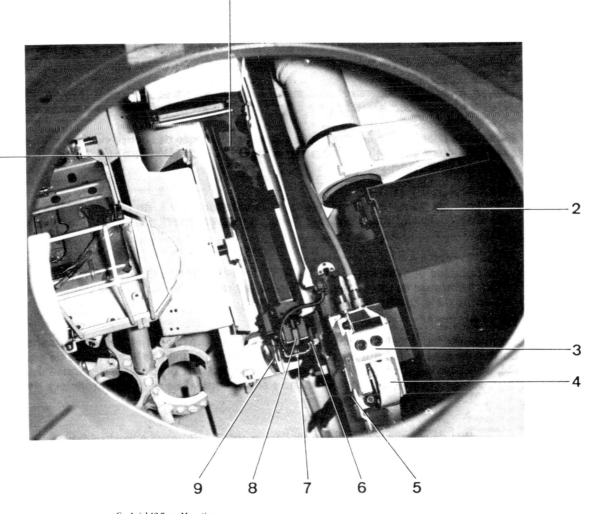

Co-Axial 12.7mm Mounting

1. 12.7mm machinegun
2. Cn 105 F-1 breech
3. Loader's fire authorization warning light
4. Loader's 105mm gun safety contact lever
5. Loader's 105mm gun safety contact lever lock
6. Co-axial machine gun mechanical firing lever
7. Locking lever
8. Electrical firing switch
9. Cocking lever
10. 12.7mm ammunition feed

The 12.7mm co-axial machine gun was a weapon many experienced AMX-30B crewmen were sad to see replaced by the 20mm CN20 F2 as a retrofit to the AMX-30B fleet in the late 1970s and in the new AMX-30B2. Here we can see how the 12.7mm co-axial weapon was fitted to the base of the CN 105 F1 breech, which explained why the weapon's barrel did not protrude through the mantlet. Since the weapon was for all intents an M2 Browning, it was a reliable and well-regarded weapon. [Thomas Seignon]

ing gear changing procedure to master. Once a driver had the feel for the gear changing process, the AMX-30B eventually endeared itself to most of its drivers.

The training center at Carpiagne maintained a small fleet of driver training tanks without turrets, in order to ensure that conscript tank drivers could be provided with the best possible training for this task. These training tanks allowed the instructors to regularly change drivers throughout a training session. The CIABC also kept a fleet of regular AMX-30B gun tanks to train the drivers in maneuvering the tank with its long gun in confined spaces and to learn to steer the tank without banging the main armament into trees or buildings. Conscript and volunteer drivers alike were trained at Carpiagne.

With the requirement for night time operation and combat the driver was expected to master driving with the use of infra-

red periscopes. The driver had to always be mindful of the turret position, and to engage his hydraulic traverse cut out switch when driving head out, because sudden traverse with the gun depressed could cause the driver serious injury. In combat the driver would have stood little chance in the event of a close range hit on the front of the hull resulting in penetration of the glacis plate, with half the tank's main armament ammunition and some of the diesel fuel stored to his immediate right. The intention of the design was to maximise the use of the AMX-30's high power to weight ratio to permit quick accelerations from position to position, which in essence became the driver's main responsibility.

The driver and other crew members could also be expected to be trained for submerged river crossings. These began with specially constructed cisterns and graduated to actual crossings of large ponds and eventually river beds. The experience must

The AMX-32, designed by GIAT from 1975 as a possible successor to the AMX-30B. Two prototypes were built, in 1979 and 1981. The French Army never bought the AMX-32, and had already ordered the improvement program that came to be known as the AMX-30B2 by 1980. The AMX-32 was an all-welded vehicle armoured with a steel armour system employing plates of differing hardness, a COTAC fire control system and the DIVT-13 low light camera. Here we can see the 1981 prototype, which featured a more angular mantlet. [Thomas Seignon]

An official publicity photograph of the 1981 prototype of the AMX-32, seen here with its lot de bord and with its crew in this GIAT publicity photograph. [*Nexter Systems/Collection du Musé des Blindés de Saumur*]

An official GIAT publicity photograph of the 1979 prototype of the AMX-32, which more closely followed the lines of the AMX-30. [*Nexter Systems/Collection du Musé des Blindés de Saumur*]

Official publicity photograph of one of the AMX32 prototypes. The AMX-32 was offered to customers for several years and amongst other sub-systems, several transmissions were extensively tested during its evaluation by GIAT and the AMX engineers at Satory. [*Nexter Systems/Collection du Musé des Blindés de Saumur*]

The AMX-10RC was a powerfully armed reconnaissance vehicle developed from the mid-1970s by GIAT to replace the Panhard EBR. It was from the AMX-10RC's advanced COTAC fire control system and the kinetic ammunition designed for its CN 105 F2 gun that the basic improvements incorporated in the AMX-30B2 program's turret systems were borrowed. [Lionel Gonnet]

At least one AMX-30B hull carried the special T142 ACRA turret and was tested between 1970 and 1974. Much like contemporary Soviet and American missile tank projects, the ACRA project sought to provide a long range antitank capability through the use of a combined gun/launcher system. The concept was similar to that adopted in the American M60A2 and M551 Sheridan (armed with the 152mm Shillelagh system). The complete 142mm round weighed 20 Kg and had a theoretical maximum range of 8000 metres (although from the layout of the turret the elevation would not have been sufficient to enable such a long range). The ACRA missile itself weighed 26 kg and had a range of 3300 metres, could be fired at 4 rounds per minute, and could penetrate 380mm of armour plate. The ACRA, with nearly 10 years of development and funding invested, was dropped in favour of the less expensive HOT missile in 1974. This turret is all that remains of the AMX-30 ACRA today, stocked in the yard of the Saumur *Musée des Blindées*. [P. Besson]

have been best described as frightening in a tank with as many reliability problems as the early AMX-30B. The AMX-30B was built from the assembly line as a sealed unit, and preparing the tank for submerged crossings was a simple task included within the tank's design parameters from the start. The *Arme Blindée Cavalerie* eventually developed a complete doctrine for submerged crossing by armoured regiments, with a well versed training organization to support every aspect of the submerged crossing process. A crossing was always assisted by engineer divers with a communications officer from the bank. The divers were known as *Plongeurs d'Aide de Franchissement*, or PAFs, and were tasked with identifying suitable fords and crossing points. PAF divers were elite troops drawn from the corps of engineers, who were often parachute qualified. To them fell the task of assisting stranded submerged vehicles and assuring their safe recovery. The PAF divers were trained to rescue crewmen from stranded vehicles. During a crossing, a PAF team floating above the crossing area in a zodiac provided a running commentary of the submerged tank's progress, and submerged crossings were always supported by a recovery team to winch any breakdowns out immediately with an AMX-30D. The main risk during submerged crossings was always engine failure, which could happen if water was aspirated by the engine through any leaks in the various hatch seals that assured the impermeability of the engine compartment. The exhaust pipe covers were another point where water could easily find a way in, with consequent risk of drowning the engine.

Submersion towers of several heights fixed to the loader's hatch were available for training. For combat use the narrow combat schnorkel was fixed to the loader's periscope aperture, which permitted crossings in water as deep as four meters. In

The Leopard 1A5, an upgrade very similar in spirit to the AMX-30B2. The fire control system developed for the Leopard 2 in this case was adapted to suit the older L7 105mm gun fitted to the original Leopard 1 turret, and while never implemented, the feasibility of refitting the entire Leopard 1 fleet with the new Rheinmetal 120mm gun was proven as part of the program. [Jurgen Scholz]

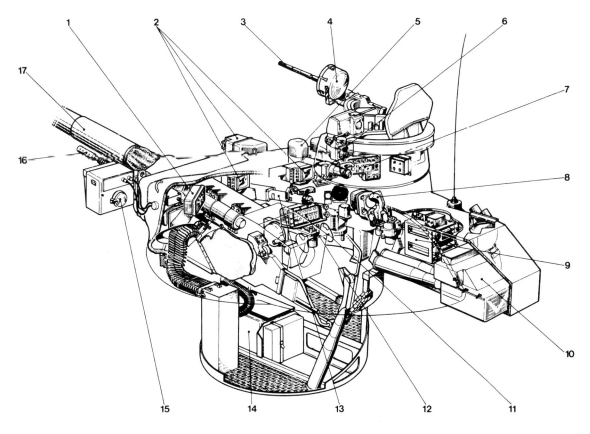

AMX-30B2 Turret, General Layout (early vehicle)

1. Loader's display panel
2. DIVT-13A low light camera system (system and monitors)
3. AAN 7.62mm cupola machine gun mounting
4. PH-9A cupola infrared searchlight
5. Commander's M496 sight
6. TJN 223
7. Commander's display panel
8. Commander's traverse and elevation control
9. Wireless installation
10. NBC system and ventilation unit
11. Gunner's traverse and elevation control
12. Gunner's display panel
13. M581 gun sight
14. Turret main electrical junction box
15. PH-8B infrared/white light search light
16. Cn 20 F2 20mm co-axial cannon
17. Cn 105 F1 105mm main armament

The layout of the AMX-30B2's turret systems. The NBC system was moved to the rear of the turret bustle on the exterior of the turret, and we can see the bulky feed system for the CN 20 F2 and location of the radios. [Thomas Seignon]

The *Wagram*, an AMX-30B of the *2e Escadron 501e RCC*, wearing the temporary disruptive camouflage scheme carried by the thirteen tanks of the 2/501eRCC on deployment to Senegal in 1982. This was the only occasion that French AMX-30Bs were ever deployed outside of France's NATO commitments. Because in 1982 the *2e Escadron* was the only professionalised squadron of tanks in the entire *Arme Blindée Cavalerie*, the political implications of this first foreign deployment were minimal (an issue revisited during Operation *Daguet*, nearly a decade later). *Wagram*, like *Austerlitz*, was a battle honour shared by many French regiments, and was used as a *nom de baptême* in many units. (B. Bidault with thanks to C. Legrand)

the early 1970s, AMX-30B-equipped armoured regiments in the *Forces Francaises en Allemagne* placed great importance on submerged crossing in the annual training schedule. Because river lines criss-crossed so much of the potential battlefield in central Europe, and enemy bridge demolition was assumed as a matter of course, submerged crossing offered a quicker means of river crossing than waiting for engineers to bridge rivers under fire. It was considered a critical task for at least a full *peloton* in each *escadron* to be proficient in submerged crossing in each *régiment blindé*, and the process always received due publicity within the army. Schnorkel operations for submerged river crossings were regularly practised right until the late 1990s.

An early AMX-30B2 being unloaded during tank transporter trials in the mid 1980s. [Jacques Maillard]

An early AMX-30B2 photographed in the mid-1980s, as can be deduced by the M65 crew helmets. [Francis Cany]

Submerged crossings, though a rite of passage for AMX-30 crews, were not the only means by which river crossings were addressed by the French Army. The post-war experience of fighting in the colonies and the importance of river crossing operations in 1944-45 had driven a thorough approach to solving river crossing problems and explains the weight given to

submerged crossing capabilities in the AMX-30B specification. The *Pont Gillois* was a second such solution.

The Gillois mechanised ferries employed by the French Army's *Genie* (Engineers) at divisional level were models of the type, and remained in service for many years. The army also deployed the bridgelaying AMX-13 *Poseur de Pont*, although

A lineup of AMX-30B2 tanks ready for a major parade in the 1980s. They carry the earlier DIVT-13 low light camera, standard on all AMX-30B2s built or converted before 1988-1989. [Francis Cany]

The 503e RCC lined up for official inspection in August 1986. [Jacques Maillard]

the latter bore a bridge too lightly rated to carry an AMX-30 series vehicle, and a standard AMX-30 *Poseur de Pont* never entered service in any numbers. Some of the massive Gillois vehicles could be combined to carry three AMX-30B or AMX-30B2 gun tanks at the same time whilst crossing a major water course, and drivers had to master placing their tanks on these monsters carefully to not affect the Gillois' trim in the water. Another task for the driver to master involved getting a battle tank onto the trailer of the large Berliet *Porte Char* (tank transporter) or onto the railway flats of the SNCF or *Deutsche Bahn* for transport to and from training areas. Both demanded skill and close communications with the logistics troops who

conducted these operations on a daily basis in some instances. As in any tank, the AMX-30 driver had a heavy workload and good drivers were highly valued. Perhaps as recognition that his tank was a demanding vehicle to drive, in most regiments AMX-30B drivers were not expected to do night guard duty whilst on manoeuvres.

The periodic mechanical problems common to the AMX-30B were taxing to the driver, and engine overheating and transmission failures were common, especially in the early part of the AMX-30B's career. One of the critical drills the driver had to master quickly was the shut-down procedure, which took about fifteen minutes of idling the main fan revolutions per

The 503e RCC's regimental command tank passes in review. [Jacques Maillard]

A freshly painted AMX-30B2 of the *4ᵉ Régiment de Dragons* (4e RD), received from 1984 onwards. The occasion for the new paint job was the regiment's participation in the 1986 Bastille Day parade. At this time the 3 colour disruptive camouflage scheme was not yet universally adopted. We can however see the new tactical marking system had been adopted by the 4ᵉ RD. The tank is that of the *sous officier adjoint* (equivalent to a troop sergeant) of the *1e Peloton, 3e Escadron*. The triangle marking represents the *3ᵉ Escadron*, the vertical bar the *1ᵉ Peloton*, and the central position of the horizontal bar represents the second in command's tank. The empty 20mm F2 ammunition box being employed as a stowage box as seen here was a practice so widespread that it was almost official. [Thomas Seignon]

Some of the features seen on true new production AMX-30B2 tanks included the new thickened mantlet and cast turret without range-finder openings. We can see the bulged gunner's sight cover and the DIVT-13 mounting. This tank, going by the *immatriculation*, was newly built in 1984. It is uncertain how many new B2 mantlets and turrets were cast by the Atelier de Tarbes. This tank is not carrying its battery hatch covers in the stowed position on the glacis, and was photographed in its hangar. [Thomas Seignon]

This AMX-30B2 of the *2ᵉ Escadron, 1ᵉ Régiment de Dragons* on maneuvers in open terrain. With his head outside his hatch, the driver's vision is much improved but prevents rotation of the turret because of the use of driver's traverse cut-off switch. The air recognition panel wrapped around the gun barrel was one of two double-sided types carried, allowing the selection of red, pink, orange and yellow. These panels were frequently used during exercises to determine unit identity. [Thomas Seignon]

minute slowly downwards. An abrupt engine shutdown risked the cooling fan's blades shattering with grievous consequences to the hydraulic hoses and oil lines in the engine compartment. Even in the later part of the 1970s the incidence of power pack changes could be frequent and the regiment's AMX-30D recovery vehicles were at times hard pressed to keep up with breakdowns. When the tank was in good mechanical order the driver trained hard at charging from one fire position to the next on the training ground at the commander's orders. French

doctrine stressed high speed in the attack and to avoid enemy fire, but the AMX-30's fire control system was designed to shoot at the halt. The AMX-30B was amongst the fastest and lightest vehicles of its type, and with its stiff suspension, it always meant a bumpy ride for the crews.

The use of the M208 optical rangefinder and fire control system by the turret crew were practised and assessed at set times in the training year with the luxury of live firing on ranges with live ammunition being closely controlled for budgetary reasons.

An AMX-30B2 climbing onto a Nicolas tank transporter trailer pulled by the Berliet TRH 350 tractor unit. The tank is equipped with a SIMFIRE fixed to the gun barrel behind the air recognition panel. It also carries an STC combat fire simulator with flashing lights secured on the turret baskets. [Thomas Seignon]

Probably photographed in the late 1980s, a fine view of two AMX-30B2s undergoing engine maintenance. The *Dunkerque* has the engine decking and rear plates removed. The rear plate on the AMX-30B2 was substantially different from the AMX-30B and the infantry telephone box was moved to a central position. [Thomas Seignon]

Winching off the rear plate on the AMX-30B2 was an essential step to a pack lift or transmission repairs, just like the older AMX-30B. The powerpack could be changed as one unit in about an hour and a half with an experienced AMX-30D crew. [Thomas Seignon]

The gunner employed an M271 telescopic sight for daylight use and an infra-red OB17A sight for use in night operations. Each regiment was put through its paces in the annual autumn NATO manoeuvres, which was the climax of every training year in the *Arme Blindé Cavalerie* as it was in all other NATO armies. The AMX-30B's turret was laid out ergonomically and a rapid rate of fire was possible, with roughly half the available 47 rounds of main armament ammunition in racks in the turret bustle. Up to three TRVP13A or TRVP213B wireless sets could be fitted, operated by the commander and loader, and incorporating the crew intercom system. A squadron or regimental command tank could be identified by three antennas on the turret roof, while a platoon command tank had two, and a standard battle tanks only carried a single antenna.

A tactical marking based on the NATO armoured unit symbol was carried on the front left and rear right mudguards on nearly all AMX-30 series gun tanks from the late 1970s onwards. The unit is identified on the left side, the formation on the right. Here we see a marking seen on an AMX-30B2 Brennus photographed in the early 2000s, from the *1e-2e Regiment de Chasseurs*, of the *7e Brigade Blindée*. [Pierre Delattre]

The DIVT-13 mounting was more rectangular and lacked the semi-circular guard seen on the face of the later DIVT-16 thermal gunnery camera. [Pierre Delattre]

This AMX-30B2 has been converted into a *Char École*, a special driver training tank as employed at the Carpiagne training center. This first derivative of the AMX-30 family was based on both AMX-30B, and much later as in the case of this example, on AMX-30B2s. [Thomas Seignon]

The rear view of the AMX-30B2 *Char École* shows the changes in layout on the hull rear plate as a result of the new transmission, which made driving a much easier and less tiring experience. [Thomas Seignon]

The AMX-30B2

In the 1970s the AMX-30B was recognized by the troops as a basically good design, sometimes let down by its power train. The principal weakness of the AMX-30B's mechanical design had always been the AMX 5-SD-200D transmission. A number of incremental production improvements were introduced during the course of the AMX-30B's production at the *Atelier de Roanne* in the late 1970s, but a comprehensive modernization of the 30-ton tank was ignored in favour of other priorities. The most vis-

The AMX-40 MBT was a second major effort after the failure of the AMX-32 to attract export sales for GIAT in the mid-1980s. With much of the sales effort directed towards the Saudi Arabian armed forces, the AMX-40 was a new design based on a larger sized chassis and armed with a 120mm gun. The AMX-40 was still much smaller than the Challenger, M1 or Leopard 2, and carried only 36 rounds of 120mm ammunition. Ultimately, the design owed much to the AMX-30 series and it failed to sell. [Thomas Seignon]

A second view of the GIAT AMX-40, which weighed some 43 tonnes and employed heavier armour than the AMX-32. A smoothbore 120mm that fired 120mm Rheinmetal ammunition was provided as the main armament. Only 3 AMX-40 prototypes were built by GIAT in 1983, 1984 and 1985. The French army skipped this entire development stage of MBT design, holding on to the AMX-30B2 until the late 1990s before the introduction of the very technologically advanced Leclerc. [Thomas Seignon]

ible modernization was the replacement of the 12./mm co-axial armament with the 20mm F2 cannon from about 1976, which was also installed at unit level as a *programme de valorisation* or update program on many of the earlier production vehicles. In 1979 the AMX-30B2 officially began as a design study at GIAT. The AMX-30B2 program that eventually followed involved at first the production of a brand new tank. Three main improvements were incorporated into the AMX-30B2, relating to the power pack, the gun and fire control system. The program was amended to become a comprehensive factory rebuild program of the existing AMX-30B fleet after 1984.

By 1979 the AMX-30B suffered from the lack of a modern fire control system, and from the lack of a kinetic energy round

for the 105mm F1 gun. The gun itself was still well regarded within the army, and so the new munitions and fire control technology standardized during the GIAT AMX-10RC's development allowed the AMX-30B's turret systems to be comprehensively modernised using proven technology. The AMX-10RC

An official publicity photograph of the AMX40, showing some of the features that made it stand apart from the earlier French battle tank designs. The panoramic sights, integral dozer blade, 12 road wheels, 6 barrelled smoke dischargers and 120mm smoothbore gun were all modern features. Sadly the design was still rooted in the concept of the earlier 30 and 32 ton battle tanks in a new era of 60-ton MBTs with composite armour. [*Nexter Systems/Collection du Musé des Blindés de Saumur*]

An official publicity photograph of the AMX40 taken at one of the Satory arms show in the mid 1980s. [*Nexter Systems/Collection du Musé des Blindés de Saumur*]

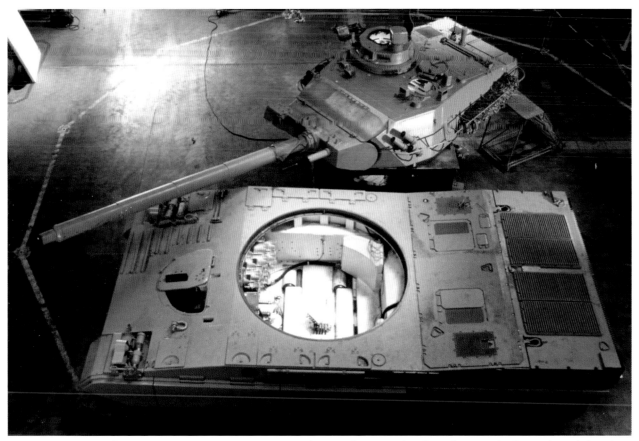

This official publicity photograph show an AMX-40 prototype with turret dismounted in the mid-1980s. The design showed clean lines and modern features, and was aimed at the export market. France waited another dozen years before the AMX-30's successor was adopted, in the form of the heavier and far more capable Leclerc. [*Nexter Systems/Collection du Musé des Blindés de Saumur*]

was one of the most modern and heavily armed wheeled AFVs when it entered service in 1976 and it shared enough characteristics with the AMX-30B's basic armament to allow GIAT to develop improvements for the AMX-30 at relatively low risk and with low development costs.

The AMX-32 battle tank developed at AMX (Satory) between 1975 and 1981 had incorporated the AMX-10RC's fire control system in a battle tank successfully, and served as a second template for upgrading the AMX-30B. The AMX-32 was a modernized AMX-30B for all intents, and its design incorporated a new welded hull and turret, employing an armour system that relied on advanced metallurgy (and its armour included plates of varying hardness). Its armour represented a large advance in terms of protection over the traditional ho-

The AMX-30B2's night vision capabilities were upgraded considerably by the introduction of the Thales DIVT-16 Castor thermal gunnery camera in 1988. This is the prototype DIVT-16 equipped AMX-30B2 at the Saumur Carousel in 1988 wearing an unusual camouflage scheme. Although the Castor system was a major upgrade, it did not change the AMX-30B2's designation and was fitted to tanks rebuilt from 1988-1989 onwards, at first alongside conversions being fitted with the earlier DIVT-13. [P. Besson]

The AMX-30B was also used in the development of the ECP program (*Engin Principal de Combat*) which would become the AMX-56, or Leclerc MBT. This particular vehicle has been reconfigured with sheet metal fairings to lessen the vehicle's heat signature. [Thomas Seignon]

mogenous welded or cast armour steel of the AMX-30B in a 40 ton battle tank, but despite extensive testing of the two prototypes built by GIAT in 1979 and 1981, the AMX-32 was not adopted by the French Army.

The AMX-30B2 improvement program included the improvement of the AMX-30's power pack, beginning with the replacement of the original transmission with the new Minerva SESM ENC-200 semi-automatic type incorporating hydrostatic steering. The new transmission allowed the tank to be driven with a steering wheel instead of the original two stick system found on the AMX-30B. While the Hispano-Suiza diesel was judged an adequate basic design, an improved version (designated HS-110-2), with new turbo-compressors was adopted for the B2. This gave a 45 horsepower increase over the original

The turret front of a later AMX-30B2 conversion with the DIVT-16 CASTOR camera fitted. The DIVT-16 CASTOR was a great improvement on the already successful DIVT-13 low light camera and gave the AMX-30B2 true thermal gunnery capabilities from 1988-89 onwards. The CASTOR was however expensive and relatively few conversions fitted with the new system were available until the early 1990s. [Pierre Delattre]

Two more AMX-30B2s on exercise in Champagne, probably just after the end of the cold war. The AMX-30B2 was really intended to shoot from the halt, although it could shoot on the move with a reduction in accuracy. By the early 1990s many of these tanks stopped carrying the PH-8B searchlight on exercise, and the stowage location on top of the turret bustle bin was often taken up with other stowage arrangements more particular to individual crews. The PH-8B was however carried on active operations in 1991. [Thomas Seignon]

The tank commander, and his machine. The tactical marking indicates the third tank, *1e Peloton*, although the mechanical availability of machines often dictated who operated which tank in the real world! The number 5 in the white disc with 2 red dots next to the tank's name *Oeully* are SNCF rail embarcation codes. The number 5 indicated a special transport wagon and the 2 red dots indicated an oversized load. [Thomas Seignon]

HS-110 engine. The new power pack, like the original, could be changed as a single unit in 45 minutes using an AMX30D recovery vehicle. The mechanical issues which had been a serious problem with the original AMX-30B tanks had gradually begun to disappear as component manufacture improved, but they ceased almost entirely after many of the AMX-30 fleet were rebuilt to B2 standard. A large number of the AMX-30 derivatives eventually also received the new Minerva transmission, but these upgraded vehicles did not change in basic designation.

The development of composite armour systems like the Chobham system, and the adoption of spaced and laminated armour systems in the Soviet Union also presented a major problem to the AMX-30B. The *Obus-G* was no longer considered as the AMX-30's silver bullet by the late 1970s. By 1980-82 the adoption of reactive armour on many Soviet MBTs (including numbers of the older T62 and T55 medium tanks) also demanded that a kinetic energy round be developed for the CN 105 F-1.

The CN 105 F-1 gun received a new Armour Piercing Fin Stabilised Discarding Sabot (APFSDS or *Obus Flêche*) round with a range of 1700 metres to improve the tank's anti-armour capabilities, and the AMX-30B2 retained the 20mm F-2 co-axial weapon. The new COTAC fire control system was that already proven on the AMX-10RC, which GIAT claimed could give a 99% chance of a hit under ideal conditions. The COTAC system incorporated the APX M581.03A sight with laser range-finder for the gunner, the APX M579 electronic gun control system and the APX M421 optical module. The gunner was also provided with a traversable M282 periscope and retained the original design's M223 fixed episcopes in the turret wall.

The COTAC system included trunnion tilt sensors and determined range with the CILAS APX M550 laser range finder and

1991, south of the large base at Mailly in eastern France. The eastern part of France, with its many military bases, was a huge training area every autumn for much of the cold war. The ground in Champagne turns into a morass of chalky mud as soon as rain hits it, and under its muddy coat the 3 tone camouflage on these AMX-30B2s of the *1e Régiment de Cuirassiers* can hardly be seen. [Thomas Seignon]

With the turret trained to 9 o'clock we can see the long gun barrel on this AMX-30B2. The flashing lights and the warning triangle on the rear jerrycan rack suggest that this tank was photographed off base in open country. [Thomas Seignon]

Operation Daguet. Some 40 AMX-30B2s of the *4e Régiment de Dragons* participated in the liberation of Kuwait as the spearpoint of the 6e DLB. [D. Rotaris]

upgrades to the sights for aiming the new OFL rounds. The old optical rangefinder apertures on converted vehicles were simply covered by blanking plates. Night fighting capability was improved by the provision of a DIVT-13 low light television camera system as standard equipment on all the early AMX-30B2s. Low Light Television Cameras are photon-sensitive optical systems that pick up wavelengths of light above the visible spectrum (0.4 to 0.7 micrometers) from minimal levels of ambient light. These systems use the principle of image-intensification (employing vidicon tubes and multiplier tubes to gather and concentrate ambient light) to create a visible image for night vision.

The Thomson CSF Sagem DIVT-13 system (DIVT being an acronym for *Dispositif d'Intensification pour la Visée et le Tir*) had appeared on the AMX-10RC armoured car in the 1976-77 period and was already tried and tested by the time it was

A tired looking AMX-30B2 of the *4e Régiment de Dragons* photographed after the regiment's return from *Operation Daguet,* with sand and brown paint worn completely off in some places. [Francis Cany]

included in the AMX-30B2 upgrade program. The DIVT 13 had a range of 1300 meters which was an improvement on the earlier infra-red system used on the AMX-30B. A system based on similar principles to the DIVT-13 equipped the first batches of Leopard 2 tanks procured by the Bundeswehr in 1979-1980.

The commander's original TOP7 cupola's binocular sight was replaced by the OB49 combined day/night sight and the

M496 secondary sight. All of the commander's optical devices permitted direct engagement with both main and secondary armament by the AMX-30B2's commander. The loader also was provided with an M282 periscope and retained the original two fixed M223 episcopes. Provision was also made for the OB31A image intensification periscope for the driver, which could be swapped for the central periscope of the standard triple

A rear ¾ view of another returned veteran from Operation Daguet. This tank has the large mantlet searchlight fitted, still painted in *Vert Armée.* The rear of the turret has several additional stowage boxes fitted. [Francis Cany]

Preserved at Mailly and photographed in 2007, a rather pristine AMX-30B2 in the colours of the *4e Regiment de Dragons* as worn in the 1991 Gulf War. Much as with the British Army's deployment of the Challenger 1 to the gulf, the *Arme Blindée Cavalerie* had to scrape together enough Castor-equipped B2s to send a 44 tank regiment, but the need to send only professional soldiers for political reasons also caused the need to temporarily transfer the *2e Escadron* of the 501e RCC to the 4e RD. [Pierre Delattre]

This AMX-30B2, forgotten in a fenced compound and awaiting its fate, is possibly a Gulf War veteran from Operation *Daguet*. The unusual feature for a *Daguet* tank is that it is fitted with the DIVT-13 system, so if indeed it was brought to the Gulf in 1991, it was likely a reserve vehicle. [Thomas Seignon]

Maneuvers were often combined with range drill periods in the *Arme Blindée Cavalerie*. Here some AMX-30B2s of the *1e Regiment de Cuirassiers* are seen in one such drill period photographed in the early 1990s. The different range flags can all be seen: green indicates a tank ready to fire, red a tank in the course of firing, orange a firing incident. The white X on the tank in the foreground is the indicative of a squadron commander's tank in the marking system adopted after 1986, as do the two radio antennae on the turret. [Thomas Seignon]

The *507e Régiment de Chars de Combat*, seen here on a night exercise at Fontevraud in 1995, was for many years one of the dedicated training regiments of the *Arme Blindée Cavalerie*. This AMX-30B2 carries the PH-8B searchlight. [P. Besson]

The 507e RCC was one of the Saumur training units for many years. Here we can see AMX-30B2s in the Fontevraud area in March 1995. The crews are preparing their vehicles for nocturnal operations, and the DIVT-16 Castor system is about to come into its element. [P. Besson]

Another scene from the 507e RCC training exercise in March 1995 at Fontevraud. This AMX-30B2 is being refueled, filling the front fuel tank. The tank pictured still carries the PH-8B searchlight. [P. Besson]

M223 observation periscope arrangement used for driving the tank closed down. Other upgrades included an armoured jacket for the AA NF-1 7.62mm cupola machine gun. The resulting improvements brought the AMX-30B2's all up weight to 37 tons, necessitating a suspension upgrade, so the original pattern of torsion bars was replaced with a larger diameter type used on some of the AMX-30 support vehicles.

By 1980 some sixty four new AMX-30B2 tanks were on order. The 503e RCC tested out the AMX-30B2 prototypes in 1981. The prototypes were modified AMX-30B tanks fitted with the new turret systems, the improved HS-110-2 engine and the automatic Minerva transmission. The experience of integrating the new fire controls and laser rangefinder envisaged for the AMX-30B2 in the AMX-10RC's turret (which employed the very similar CN 105 F-2, a lightened version of the F-1 gun) made the development of the AMX-30B2 pass quickly and successfully to the production stage.

The Mourmelon training ground in 1995. The unit seen is the *2e Régiment de Chasseurs*, who later received the AMX-30B2 Brennus. They were amalgamated with the *1e Régiment de Chasseurs* in 1996. The *1e RCh* were a former training regiment which had maintained a diverse fleet of vehicles including the AMX-10RC, AMX-30B and after 1982, the AMX-30B2. [P. Besson]

This AMX-30B2 of the 2e RCh was photographed at La Chaume in 1995. It is likely an early vehicle with the AMX-30B2's purpose built cast turret. Confirmed figures for the actual number of AMX-30B2s built and converted are still unclear, but at the end of 1996 one report quoted the French Army's tank fleet at 148 Leclerc MBTs on strength and some 658 AMX-30B2s. Since the *2e Régiment de Dragons* and the RIMECA companies still had AMX-30Bs on strength into 1997, these figures are likely incomplete. [P. Besson]

The ultimate purpose of the AMX-30B2 program seems to have concentrated on the possibility of rebuilding the existing French Army AMX-30B tanks to the improved standard at minimal cost. This was a compromise with political connotations; an economically more desirable solution than simply buying more new tanks, but one which still kept the Roanne plant in production. This AMX-30B2 requirement was theoretically supposed to be extended to over 1040 tanks rebuilt to the B2 standard by GIAT. The total number of all AMX-30B2s completed (newly built AMX-30B2s combined with the AMX-30B2 conversions) was much smaller. This was mainly because the Roanne plant could only modernize a certain number of vehicles in a given year, and was still producing other weapon systems. There was also the matter of funding for the conversions (which included expensive sub-systems like the gunnery cameras). Funding for the AMX-30B2 conversion program was curtailed, as part of the general reduction expected for the *Arme Blindée Cavalerie* after the Cold War ended. The conversion of existing AMX-30B into AMX-30B2 at the *Atelier de Roanne* ceased in 1993 with the final order of 92 conversions being cancelled.

The *2e Régiment de Chasseurs* in 1995 on the Mourmelon training ground. [P. Besson]

The AMX-30B2 was fully capable of submerged river crossings just like the older AMX-30B. This tank of the 2e RCh is about to cross the river Marne in 1995. [P. Besson]

The AMX-30B2 employed the exact same combat snorkel as used by the AMX-30B. Here the AMX-30B2 seen in the preceding photo emerges on the far bank of the Marne. [P. Besson]

Hatches open, a sigh of relief for this crew, who will not need to be rescued by the PAF team. We can see that as a precaution, the towing hawsers were already fitted in the event that a recovery would have been needed. This tank is an early AMX-30B2, with the new cast turret pattern and the DIVT-13 camera system. [P. Besson]

On the opposite bank, the tank pictured has just emerged from the crossing point. [P. Besson]

MDL Cabedoce is the name of this tank of the *2e Régiment de Chasseurs' 4e Escadron*. The MDL stands for *Maréchal de Logis*, the French Cavalry's equivalent rank to a sergeant. In many regiments, tanks were named after the battles and provinces of France, or after the regiment's fallen from the first or second world wars. [P. Besson]

Prior to the crossing, the regiment's tanks wait in an assembly area for their turn to cross the Marne. [P. Besson]

The *4e Escadron* of the *2e Régiment de Chasseurs*, lined up in 1995 for their turn at the Marne crossing. [P. Besson]

The AMX-30B2 model addressed many of the AMX-30B's known weaknesses but it made no effort to re-examine the question of the AMX-30's original light armour protection, a question of some relevance now that the tank was expected to conduct engagements at 1200-1500 metres with kinetic energy rounds. Despite the AMX-32 programs' efforts to improve the basic protection of the vehicle using welded steel plates of varying hardness, the AMX-30B2 program retained the cast steel turret and the existing hull design of the AMX-30B. In the new era of composite armour the AMX-30B2 still only carried a maximum of 81mm thick steel frontal armour. The AMX-

30B2 emerged as a better combat vehicle than the AMX-30B, but remained a substantially less capable battle tank than the M1 Abrams, Leopard 2A4 and Challenger 1 second generation MBTs due to its less powerful gun and its original steel armour. Despite this fact, the tactical formations devised to field the AMX30B2 offset some of the vehicle's qualitative disadvantages. In comparison to most of the NATO's older MBTs the AMX-30B2 stood as a perfectly adequate design and was superior to many. The new AMX-30B2 modifications enabled the AMX-30 to substantially fulfill its mission according to French requirements for the foreseeable future. From 1982 it was simply a matter of getting enough AMX-30B2s into service.

The AMX-30B2 order was increased to 166 tanks and then to 271 vehicles for the French Army, and the conversions program continued hereafter. The only special purpose variant of the AMX-30B2 was the specialised engineer vehicle, the

The *Wagram*'s turret has been lifted off and we can see the turret basket. The regiment's staff have blue hard hats on and the crowd is held back by barriers for safety in best peace time fashion. The AMX-30D remains a standard vehicle in the French Army to this day, a batch having recently been rebuilt as a standard support vehicle for the new Nexter VBCI infantry combat vehicle. [Lionel Gonnet]

After 1995, many of France's remaining armoured regiments were amalgamated as the army shrank and the new Leclerc MBT made its appearance in increasing numbers. Here we can see an open day at the Olivet base in 1997 where the *6e-12e Cuirassiers* were stationed. The new Leclerc had yet to completely replace all the regiment's tanks and here we can see an older AMX-30B2, the *Wagram*, having its turret removed as part of a public display. [Lionel Gonnet]

Another view of the Wagram's turret, from the side this time. By 1997 the AMX-30B2 Brennus conversions had entered service as the rest of the ABC's AMX-30B2 fleet awaited retirement. It was only the slow deliveries of the Leclerc which kept the AMX-30B2 on strength at this time. [Lionel Gonnet]

The Cypriot National Guard operates some 54 AMX-30B2s alongside Russian T-80U MBTs in the 20th Armoured Brigade. [Stelios Markides]

A Cypriot National Guard AMX-30B2 during crew training. Note the use of the crimson air recognition panel spread over the turret bustle bin. [Stelios Markides]

An overhead view of a Cypriot National Guard AMX-30B2. [Stelios Markides]

Engin Blindé de Genie or EBG, all other AMX-30 variants having been based on the older AMX-30B. The Atelier de Tarbes produced a new turret casting without openings for the optical coincidence rangefinder fitted to the original AMX-30B turret, but a small series of these turrets were cast and they were only for the newly built AMX-30B2 series (the new turrets also had a thicker mantlet casting around the gunner's sight). The numbers of true AMX-30B2 newly built and delivered to the French Army are not absolutely clear however, because so many of the AMX-30B2 conversions were executed on older AMX-30Bs and because funding was limited. The French Defence Minister in senate proceedings in 1994 made reference to some 1079 AMX-30 series gun tanks in French Army service, comprising some 421 AMX-30Bs and 658 AMX-30B2s as the official total. Until the production figures can be confirmed, the author estimates that no more than 700 AMX-30B2s were built and converted, including the orders for the United Arab Emirates and for the Greek Cypriot National Guard.

A left rear ¾ view of a Cypriot National Guard AMX-30B2. These tanks retain the white light searchlight as well as being equipped with the DIVT-16, standard for late French AMX-30B2 conversions. [Stelios Markides]

The AMX-30B2 in Service

In January 1982 the first fifty newly built AMX-30B2 tanks were delivered to the *503e Régiment de Chars de Combat* at Mourmelon. These newly built tanks were the most modern AFVs in the French army at the time of their introduction and offered the 503e RCC much improved night fighting capabilities and a modern gunnery system. Fire on the move capability and full gun stabilisation were not design priorities to the same de-gree as seen in contemporary designs such as the Leopard 2 and M1 Abrams, but the improvements made to the tank gained it immediate popularity with the troops. The 503e RCC was given an important task as soon as its re-equipment was complete: the regiment tested out the new 1984 regimental organization being proposed to match the *Arme Blindée Cavalerie*'s new divisional structure.

The basic AMX-30B2 specification was improved during its production (or more often during its *conversion*). The most

When Greece retired her AMX-30B fleet, having ironically bought some 170 Leopard 1A5 tanks to replace them, a number of the former Hellenic Army AMX-30Bs (perhaps as many as 60 vehicles)ended up in Greek Cypriot National Guard service. [Stelios Markides]

The Cypriot National Guard still operates some 50 AMX-30B2 tanks, and the vehicles pictured here were photographed during an October 1st parade in the early 2000s. October 1st marks the celebration of the end of British rule on the island in 1960. [Stelios Markides]

Greek Cypriot National Guard AMX-30B2s and AMX-30Bs employ a number of different camouflage schemes oversprayed on top of the base sand colour. At least one study was performed for a comprehensive upgrade of the AMX-30B2s, but this was never implemented. [Stelios Markides]

important improvement came at the end of the 1980s. By the time a proper thermal sighting system was developed to supplement and replace the DIVT-13 low light television camera system on the AMX-30B2 and AMX-10RC, Thales-Sagem (later Thales Group) had become the principal contractor. The Thales DIVT-16 was a true thermal gunnery camera that was capable of thermal observation and sighting to four kilometers in daylight or in complete darkness. The DIVT-16 had an effective range in ideal conditions beyond that of the CN105-F1's accurate range with OFL munitions. Known by the acronym CASTOR (Corporate Association Sagem-Thales pour l'Optronique Révolutionnaire), the DIVT-16 was more

Rear view of a Cypriot National Guard AMX-30B2 showing its distinctive markings and standard French tools and stowage. [Stelios Markides]

expensive than the simpler DIVT-13. It was procured to retrofit on the AMX-10RC and as standard equipment on AMX-30B2 conversions from 1988 until 1992. It may also have been used to update existing AMX-30B2 tanks after the termination of the AMX-30B2 program in 1993.

The CASTOR system was at first available in small enough numbers to only be fitted to platoon commanders' tanks in each *régiment blindé* while the remainder of regiments' vehicles were

fitted with the DIVT-13 system. After 1990 the DIVT-16 replaced the DIVT-13 in new conversions completely. Both types of gunnery cameras were located on the left side of the turret outside of the armour envelope, and while an effective system, they would have been vulnerable to small arms fire and artillery fire. The later DIVT-16 CASTOR system can be visually distinguished from the earlier low-light system by the semi-circular external guard that protects the system optics, which was absent

Crewmen check over their AMX-30B2s prior to the parade, the tank in the foreground is having its suspension inspected. [Stelios Markides]

Crewmen of the 1e-2e RCh disembarking from their AMX-30B2 Brennus tanks in 1997, perhaps on their base at Thierville sur Meuse. The AMX-30B2 Brennus conversions started life with the original AMX-30B2 HS110-2 powerpack and original AMX-30 series tracks, receiving the E9 engine in 1996-1997 after Renault got the contract to re-engine the Brennus tanks and some of the artillery's AuF-1 SPGs. [Lionel Gonnet]

The first Brennus conversions were actually received by the 2e RCh and the 501e-503e RCC in 1995, before the 1e-2e RCh were amalgamated into a single RC80 type regiment. Here we can see Brennus conversions of the 2e RCh. [P. Besson]

from the more rectangular DIVT-13 mounting. Even by 1991 the number of DIVT-16 systems available in the ABC was still small, but eventually the CASTOR equipped AMX-30B2s were the last examples of the type retained in service.

The AMX-30B2 was an economical and successful way to upgrade the *Armée de Terre's* tank force; but despite its success it was not applied comprehensively to the tanks of all of France's armoured units. One or two regiments could be re-equipped with the AMX-30B2 each year. The less drastic *valorization* program was also continued in the AMX-30B fleet at unit level during the same time frame. Not all the armoured regiments had received the AMX-30B2 by the end of the Cold War. Even in the *1e Division Blindée* in Germany, older AMX-30Bs stayed

Much of the turret's frontal and side area had been taken up with the reactive armour on the Brennus conversions, which meant that the stowage carried on previous versions was relocated to the rear of the turret and to the top of the NBC box on the turret rear. This vehicle still has the original engine, and was photographed in 1997 on the base of the 1e-2e RCh. [Lionel Gonnet]

Covered in Champagne chalk, a Brennus fitted with the older model tracks (and thus very likely with the HS110 engine) sits awaiting a wash down in the first years of the Brennus' service. [Thomas Seignon]

Photographed at a public display in 1997, this Brennus has the gun sights open and the DIVT-16 CASTOR in operation. The Brennus finally gave the AMX-30B2 design a greater degree of protection. [Lionel Gonnet]

Another dirty Brennus back from the training fields of Champagne. We can see the bulk of the frontal ERA protection, and with the turret trained to the 3 o'clock position we can see that several of the ERA bricks have become detached, revealing the brackets that secured them to the turret. From examining photos of numerous Brennus conversions, the loss of ERA bricks was not uncommon. [Thomas Seignon]

in service with the *6e Régiment de Dragons*, who kept their AMX-30Bs until the regiment stood down in summer 1992. In the same division the *1e Régiment de Cuirassiers* received AMX-30B2s during the same period, which gives some clues to how the AMX-30B2 was issued, with at least one *régiment blindé* in each armoured division eventually receiving the new

tanks. Economic considerations and the fall of the Iron Curtain prevented all regiments from receiving the AMX-30B2.

A far more powerful battle tank was also developed by GIAT in the middle of the 1980s, although like the AMX-32, the AMX-40 was also never adopted by the French army. It offered a huge improvement in performance, armour and firepower over the

The commander's face covered against the dust thrown up by an armoured column, an AMX-30B2 Brennus returns to camp. [Pierre Delattre]

The following tank, which does not have a cupola machine gun fitted and is missing an ERA brick as well. [Pierre Delattre]

A dusty AMX-30B2 Brennus seen from the rear right ¾ with two crewmen resting on the turret. Without tons of kit loaded on the turret, we might surmise that the crew are awaiting a tank transporter. [Pierre Delattre]

The rear view of this AMX-30B2 Brennus shows how the rear of the turret was rearranged to accommodate the stowage that was carried on the turret sides on earlier variants. The rear hull has changed little in profile considering the addition of the more powerful Mack E9 diesel engine, which was also used on the modernized AuF-1 Self-Propelled Howitzer system. [Pierre Delattre]

This AMX-30B2 Brennus is fitted with a fire simulator system, and is covered in dry chalky Champagne mud. The Diehl tracks fitted were common to the upgraded AuF1. Interestingly, this tank is still carrying the spare track links for the first type of tracks. [Pierre Delattre]

With the turret trained towards the camera we can see how this vehicle is not fitted with an ERA brick to the right of the CN F2 20mm co-axial cannon. There are slight variations in how the ERA bricks are fitted from tank to tank. [Pierre Delattre]

Tanks of the 1ᵉ-2ᵉ Regiment de Chasseurs on the ranges towards the end of their service lives. The AMX-30B2 Brennus was withdrawn from service in 2006 and put into storage after Leclerc deliveries were completed. In recent years they have appeared on the firing ranges. [Pierre Delattre]

A side view of an AMX-30B2 Brennus taken at Thierville sur Meuse on an open day. As we can see, there was a tendency for the paint around the edges of the ERA bricks to chip off. [Jonathan Cany]

A fine view of an AMX-30B2 Brennus on an open day at Thierville sur Meuse. Again, this tank still carries the old track links. [Jonathan Cany]

AMX-30B2, but was aimed clearly at the Saudi Army when GIAT realised that French interest would fail to materialise. At 42 to 43 tons, the AMX-40 was some 13 tons lighter than a Leopard 2 and some 20 tons lighter than a Challenger 1. It employed an 1100 horsepower Poyaud diesel and composite armour for its frontal protection. Even though it used a brand new chassis with 6 road wheels on each side and a new welded turret, its AMX-30 lineage was still plain to see in the three prototypes evaluated in the mid-1980s. France had committed to the arms it already possessed, and would wait until the mid-1990s before the AMX-30B2's successor was ready to begin to take its place. GIAT failed to sell the AMX-40 to any foreign armies.

The 1984 Reorganization

Since the AMX-30B's adoption the army had adopted new divisional structures in 1967 and again in 1977. It seems in retrospect that no sooner was one tactical or strategic meta-morphosis complete than another began for the *Arme Blindée Cavalerie*. The last of the armoured regiments to convert to the AMX-30B had only started the process in the 1979-1981 period. The French 1977 pattern armoured divisions were already well balanced formations with all arms mechanised on AMX-10, AMX-13 or AMX-30 based chassis, but the army required its divisions to be more closely aligned with fighting a tactical nuclear battle well to the east of France's borders. The new 1984 reorganization allowed the reinforcement of the two French corps assigned to the defence of West Germany, largely with existing assets. It also permitted the re-equipment of the mechanised infantry, which increased the number of battle tanks in each division. This permitted a stronger army group to be kept in being for potential operations against Warsaw Pact forces, and its artillery included five Pluton nuclear SRBM regiments.

The French Army underwent a reorganization to better address the tactical problems of fighting a numerically larger enemy force. Two of France's armoured divisions (the *4e Divi-*

Exercise Azur, conducted at Châlons-en-Champagne in 2006, sets the scene for the FORAD AMX-30B2 depicted. During the exercise the *1e Brigade Mecanisée* practiced the kind of intervention that had been necessary in Kosovo in recent years. Two opposing platoons of tanks deployed in urban combat conditions. The AMX-30B2 shown has the CASTOR thermal camera system and is fitted with the DX175 simulator system. Even in 2006, some 40 years after entering service, the AMX-30 series fulfilled a valuable training function within the French Army. [Pierre Delattre]

During *Azur* 4 AMX-30B2s from the urban combat training establishment at Sissone (CENZUB) and 4 Leclerc MBTs of the *501e-503e RCC,* each supporting soldiers of the *1e Regiment d'Infanterie,* simulated deployment into the city. Local traffic was not halted in order to permit the most realistic training possible. [Pierre Delattre]

Here an AMX-30B2 commander from the CENZUB Forad contingent liaises with an infantry officer. The *nom de baptême* on this venerable AMX-30B2 is *Augueld 1805.* The FORAD unit was created from the 5e Régiment de Dragons but operated a collection of AMX-30B2s that had served in many different regiments, many of which had their original regimental markings in 2006-2007. [Pierre Delattre]

The *Augueld 1805* is fitted with the amber flashing light system mounted on the turret sides from the DX175 simulator. This particular AMX-30B2 is a rebuilt AMX-30B, as can be seen from the turret sides where the apertures for the old optical rangefinder were plated over and the welds ground smooth. [Pierre Delattre]

Another view of the plated over rangefinder aperture. Only a small series of new AMX-30B2 turrets were cast for the newly built batches of AMX-30B2 tanks bought in 1982-1984. The new tanks served alongside subsequent batches of rebuilt AMX-30B based B2s like this one. [Pierre Delattre]

Rear view of one of the CENZUB AMX-30B2s seen during *Exercise Azur*. The geometric symbol on the left side represents the *escadron*, the bar on the right represents the *peloton*. This type of turret tactical marking gradually replaced the rear bustle numbering system from 1984 onwards, often upon adoption of the 3 colour camouflage scheme. [Pierre Delattre]

An AMX-30B2 from CENTAC at Mailly. Note the Thales Castor DIVT-16 thermal camera and the wires for the pyrotechnics associated with the DX175 combat simulation system. [Pierre Delattre]

Another view of the same AMX-30B2 showing the various wires of the DX175 system. The 20mm CNF2 is not fitted. [Pierre Delattre]

The crew of this FORAD AMX-30B2 photographed at CENTAC in 2007 would have all been volunteers and included a female driver. The AMX-30 had by 2007 endured for just over four decades, encompassing a period during which much had changed in the *Armée de Terre*. [Pierre Delattre]

The tank commander of a well-worn AMX-30B2 at CENTAC in 2007 wears the later padded AFV Helmet (Casque F1 Modèle 1979) introduced in the 1980s. The majority of these tanks had the DIVT-16 camera fitted and had their NBC systems removed, revealing the rear of the turret casting. [Pierre Delattre]

Two AMX-30B2 tanks seen at CENTAC in 2007. [Pierre Delattre]

sion Blindée and the *6e Division Blindée*) were stood down. The resources necessary to support the six remaining armoured divisions in the *1e Corps d'Armée* and *2e Corps d'Armée* were reinforced from them substantially (the two corps were based at Metz and Baden respectively, and in the strictest sense only the 1e DB, 3e DB and 5e DB were stationed in the *Forces Francaises en Allemagne*). The *3e Corps d'Armée* formed a strategic reserve (and including the famous *2e Division Blindée* with regiments equipped to the RC52 standard on a somewhat lighter scale than in the other two corps) based at Lille. In time of war the *3e Corps d'Armé* would have reinforced the two corps in West Germany and eastern France. These three army corps formed

Half hidden behind a wall, an AMX-30B2 as it might have appeared in an urban combat scenario. The full simulator system is fitted and the flag flying from the radio mast is probably a CENTAC related unit flag. [Pierre Delattre]

the *Corps Blindé Mécanisé*, France's most powerfully armed postwar army group. Two new light armoured divisions were also created at the same time, along with a rapid intervention corps for use in peripheral operations or outside of France's NATO commitments. The Pluton tactical nuclear missile available since 1974 and the AuF-1 155mm self-propelled howitzer were a major part of the tactical re-orientation that was adopted to allow the French Army to fight its battle as far from French

soil as possible. For the *Arme Blindé Cavalerie* the changes coincided with the first issues of the AMX-30B2.

As far as the organization of the *régiment de chars* was affected by the army reforms of 1984, the regimental structure for an RC52 returned to the three tank squadron basis and the *escadron porté* was dropped. A mechanized *peloton* of infantry was now attached to each *escadron blindé* (an example of this organization can be seen on p.52 of *AMX-30 Char de*

This camouflaged AMX-30B2 at CENTAC in 2007 has had its NBC system removed and two large stowage boxes fitted in its stead. The red numbers on the stowage boxes denote a FORAD vehicle. [Pierre Delattre]

The pyrotechnics launcher associated with the DX175 system seen discharging on this CENTAC AMX-30B2 in 2007. [Pierre Delattre]

Well-weathered, this AMX-30B2 parked outside of its hangar at Mailly has its CN 20 F2 secondary armament demounted and the DX175 system fitted. [Pierre Delattre]

Spire 1703, seen at Mailly in 2007. The turret rear bin, housing the AMX-30B2's 1980s-era NBC system, has been removed and two stowage boxes have been substituted. One of the major consequences of the AMX-30B2's adoption of the COTAC fire control system and the various electronic components necessarily fitted inside the turret was that the NBC system had to be relocated to the turret's exterior. During the AMX-30B2 conversion the old turret stowage bin was replaced by a taller box carrying the NBC filtration system, and a new stowage box was fitted to its left side. [Pierre Delattre]

The rear plate of AMX-30B2 *Spire 1703* at CENTAC in 2007. Note how the tools and jerrycan racks have been removed. The changes to the rear plate that accompanied the new transmission and the HS110-2 upgrades are obvious without the jerrycan stowage racks and infantry phone box fitted. These tanks were training vehicles by 2007, and had been completely superseded as combat vehicles by the Leclerc MBT a year earlier. [Pierre Delattre]

Bataille 1966-2006 Volume 1). Each *escadron* was reorganized as three *pelotons* of four AMX-30B or AMX-30B2 tanks, the single *peloton* of infantry was now mounted in three VAB 4x4 wheeled armoured carriers (VAB was the acronym for *Véhicule de l'Avant Blindée* which translates to frontline armoured vehicle). The VAB carriers were armed with 7.62mm machine guns (and later with 20mm cannons). The equipment required for the new organization was not implemented completely in all regiments and priority was of course given to units in the two corps of the FFA.

Units of the *3e Corps d'Armée* based in France adopted the new 1984 system more slowly, and were given a secondary priority for receiving the AMX-30B2 and for receiving the VAB armoured personnel carriers. In the 501e RCC the *peloton porté* in each *escadron* was composed of regimental bandsmen, clerks and support personnel in the first years after the reorganization,

A CENTAC AMX-30B2 leaving the hangar area at Mailly in 2007. [Pierre Delattre]

A rather weathered AMX-30B2 at Mailly in 2007. It is fitted with the DX175 system and carries the tricolour sword *Armée de Terre* emblem adopted in the 1980s on the upper turret side (and usually applied as a decal over the plated-over rangefinder apperatures). [Pierre Delattre]

An excellent closeup of *Spire 1703*. These vehicles at CENTAC were amongst the last of the AMX-30B2 gun tanks in service, although some are used to this day by the FORAD as OPFOR vehicles. [Pierre Delattre]

Photographed at Mailly with the turret trained aft, we can see that 614-0135 has lost the two jerrycan racks, storage box and other fittings from the hull rear plate. [Pierre Delattre]

Spire 1703 photographed from the left side, sitting on the tarmac at Mailly in 2007. [Pierre Delattre]

A closeup of the left side of *Spire 1703*'s turret. The *nom de baptême* or name of the tank was given at the regimental level in the AMX-30's heyday. Many of these FORAD tanks carry the names they bore in former lives. [Pierre Delattre]

mounted in SUMB tactical vehicles and Berliet GBC 8KT trucks. In each regiment two headquarters groups formed from the *peloton de commande* operated under the regimental commander and second in command respectively. Each included an AMX-30B or AMX-30B2, a VAB communications vehicle and an AMX-10P command vehicle. At the level of the *escadron*, a command tank and VAB fulfilled the same function as a command platoon, with the rest of the command staff travelling in Hotchkiss Jeeps.

This basic 1984 RC52 regimental structure called for 52 AMX-30 series battle tanks but dispensed with tracked carriers in favour of the wheeled VAB armoured personnel carrier, partly on the grounds of economy. The availability of more powerfully armed mechanised infantry regiments arguably made the 1984 armoured divisions more versatile and powerful than the 1977

This AMX-30B2 is fitted with a drawbar for towing, and looks in rougher shape than some of the others seen at CENTAC in 2007. Note the shape of the turret rear without the bustle box fitted. Keeping the existing AMX-30B2 fleet still operating as FORAD vehicles has taken a certain degree of ingenuity in more recent years due to the dwindling stock of spares. [Pierre Delattre]

The rear contour of the turret casting is visible in this shot. The original four smoke dischargers are still fitted, which was standard for the AMX-30B2. [Pierre Delattre]

A closeup of the driver's position on 624 0046 at rest in its hangar at CENTAC. Note how the *numero d'immatriculation* is painted on in sober grey paint. The two plates carried on the left side of the glacis are fitted onto the engine decks for submerged crossing, although by 2007 such crossings would have been but a memory. By 2007 the Brennus fleet had been retired, leaving only the FORAD gun tanks operational. [Pierre Delattre]

The left side of the mantlet with the F2 20mm cannon fitted. The 20mm weapon was selected as a more powerful secondary armament that replaced the original .50 caliber (12.7mm) co-axial machinegun in the late 1970s. The choice of the 20mm weapon was theoretically as an anti-helicopter weapon, aimed from the TOP7 cupola and fired by the commander. In a more conventional ground role it was a potent anti-infantry weapon and could have theoretically knocked out a BMP at ranges of over a kilometre. Many former AMX-30B crewmen rued the day that the F2 replaced the simple old 12.7mm MG, largely because it took up more room in the turret and because its feed system was far more easily damaged. [Pierre Delattre]

The turret front with the DVT-16 Castor camera fitted. The turret optics are visible. The AMX-30 gun tanks were designed to incorporate the best possible vision devices for the commander and gunner, and the TOP7 cupola gave an excellent view of the battlefield. The AMX-30B2 program incorporated an incremental upgrade of nearly every viewing device on the tank, but the Thales DIVT-16 was perhaps the biggest leap forward employed on the design. Vision for the commander from the AMX-30 series' TOP7 is often compared favourably to the current equipment available on the Leclerc. Although this FORAD tank was photographed in 2007, the eagle insignia is that of the *5e Régiment de Cuirassiers*, the *Royal Pologne*. [Pierre Delattre]

Neerwinden, a FORAD AMX-30B2 on the training grounds at Mailly in 2007. [Olivier Carneau]

divisions. The AMX-13 VTT had been retired (except as an armoured ambulance) from the armoured regiments in 1979, in favour of the AMX10P. The 1984 program transferred the AMX-10P IFVs to the mechanised infantry allowing them to retire the older and non-amphibious AMX-13 VTT. The armoured regiments in the FFA were gradually reorganized into RC70 regiments with an fourth squadron, which had four seventeen-tank squadrons instead of the normal three seventeen-tank armoured squadron organization.

The Mechanized Infantry

Another important component of the 1984 reorganization and the adoption of the AMX-30B2 was the re-equipment of the mechanized infantry. This proceeded as tanks became available over a span of two years. Most of the mechanized infantry regiments were formed from the *Groupes de Chasseurs* (equivalent to light infantry regiments), but standard infantry regiments were also mechanized, and most of the

Despite their age, the *Neerwinden* and the other old AMX-30B2s at CENTAC and CENZUB fulfilled a valuable training mission with the French army and the FORAD crews of the old 5e Régiment de Dragons took the OPFOR role very seriously. [Olivier Carneau]

The *Neerwinden*, splattered in mud and worn from years of hard use, still hard at work on the training grounds some 40 years after the 503e RCC first took the AMX-30B on strength in 1967. [Olivier Carneau]

Some seven years have elapsed since these photos were taken in 2007, and the AMX-30B2 still serves the FORAD in dwindling numbers. [Olivier Carneau]

Many who have served on the AMX-30B2 and who went on to serve on the Leclerc look back at the AMX-30B2 as a tank that could be felt. It was a rougher ride and was a more responsive mount in the hands of a good driver. It was also considerably lighter and simpler, which had its own charm and benefits to the turret crew. [Olivier Carneau]

With the Leclerc having completely replaced the AMX-30B2 in the Arme Blindée Cavalerie as a battle tank by 2006, the AMX-30B2 still had an important training role. With the FORAD as its sole remaining user, the latter part of the first decade of the new century saw a big change in the type of markings and paint schemes carried by the old 30-ton tanks. [Olivier Carneau]

mechanized infantry regiments served in the FFA or at bases in eastern France. The AMX-30B tanks equipping these units were handed down from the *Arme Blindée Cavalerie* to replace the old AMX-13s in the organic tank companies as the AMX-30B2 was made available. At first the AMX30B simply replaced the AMX-13 light tanks in two ten-tank companies per regiment. Regiments in the FFA received two companies worth of AMX-30B, while units stationed in France only received a single such company.

In 1986 the RIMECA regimental organization changed again as more AMX-30B2s were made available to the ABC, allowing the *régiments blindés* to pass on more AMX-30Bs to the mechanized infantry, and the slightly larger escadron organization replaced the tank company within the RIMECA (although one tank was generally on loan to the RIMECA training establishment to permit a full squadron to train). Often the change from AMX-13 to AMX-30B took an entire year and this led to some very mixed tank companies in some units in the mid-1980s. Two thirteen-tank *escadrons* per mechanized regiment was then briefly the standard organization, though by the late 1980s this

changed again. Ultimately one seventeen-tank squadron mounted in AMX-30Bs and three mechanized companies mounted in AMX10P IFVs became the optimal organization for the French mechanized infantry regiments by the end of the Cold War (the RIMECA stood down their tank companies in the mid 1990s). The AMX-30B2 briefly became the ABC's most common tank type after the last AMX-30Bs were retired from the *2e Régiment de Dragons* at Couvron in 1997.

The End of the Cold War: Operation Daguet

The end of the Cold War at the end of 1989 saw many of the larger formations that composed the *Arme Blindée Cavalerie* disbanded, with the first wave of dissolutions and regimental amalgamations taking place between 1990 and 1992. To name but a few regiments, the *6e Régiment de Dragons* and *2e Régiment de Cuirassiers* disbanded during this period. The *11e Régiment de Chasseurs* in Berlin followed in 1994, and the 501e RCC was amalgamated with the 503e RCC. Many of the remaining regiments of the ABC were amalgamated in

The FORAD began maintaining vehicles in "enemy" colours in the early 2000s, at first in overall grey. The tank pictured is probably an early AMX-30B2 that has outlasted most of its contemporaries, we can see the disguised DIVT-13 low light camera and the smooth contour of what is probably one of the rarer purpose-built AMX-30B2 turrets from the 1982 to 1984 production batches. [Thomas Seignon]

The FORAD scheme best known is the grey and black striped one seen here in 2012 on the *Colonel General*. The AMX-30B2s of the FORAD were extensively disguised with sheet metal to better approximate a soviet style MBT from the mid-2000s onwards. Rear mounted fuel drums, a false schnorkel tube and even black crew uniforms. [Zurich 2RD]

the following years, as the ABC prepared to draw down to the size expected for France's post-Cold War army. The army tried to keep as many regiments in being by joining regiments and allowing each to function as a *groupe d'escadrons* of the larger whole. This was a period of transition in the army that saw many changes in equipment and in doctrine, which ultimately led to the adoption of the brigade based formations in 1999 and the disappearance of many proud units. The new Leclerc was not ready to replace the AMX-30B2 in the first half of the 1990s and about 650 AMX-30B2s remained in service long after the AMX-30B was retired.

A spectacular interlude to the AMX-30B2's further modernization came in 1991, in faraway Kuwait; *Operation Daguet*. The decision to send French troops to join the coalition forces was no simple matter, because the decision to send only professional soldiers caused grave difficulties. The 6e *Division Légere Blindée* was a wheeled formation intended for rapid deployment and did not include a tank regiment. In December 1990 there was also no single professionalized armoured regiment in the French Army's order of battle. The 501e RCC had long included a professional squadron and the *4e Régiment de Dragons* had recently established its *1e Escadron* as a completely professional

The unusual appearance of the AMX-30B2 FORAD viewed from the front. Nearly all of the AMX-30B2s still in service with the FORAD carry the DIVT-16 CASTOR camera. [Zurich 2RD]

Another view of the *Colonel General*, named for the command tank of the *5e Régiment de Dragons*, who compose the FORAD. [Zurich 2RD]

unit, which meant that the entire ABC would have to be combed for suitable personnel to form a complete regiment.

The 4e RD was assigned the mission of spearheading the 6e DLB. The *501e Régiment de Chars de Combat* seconded two officers, four Non-Commissioned Officers and eighty eight professional soldiers from its *2e Escadron* (completely professionalized since 1978) to Mourmelon to serve in the *4e RD*. These troops formed the basis for the 4e RD's *2e Escadron*, while some of the men also formed a platoon in the *3e Escadron* and others served in the *Escadron de Commandement*. The remaining positions were filled from across the rest of the ABC's regiments. A three *escadron* regiment totaling some forty AMX-30B2 tanks of the *4e Dragons* (and four tanks of the 503e RCC as reserves) then deployed to Saudi Arabia as part of the *6e Division Légère Blindée* (known as the by then as the *Division Daguet*). This was the most visible part of the French Army's contribution to the US-led coalition to liberate Kuwait from Saddam Hussein's Iraqi invasion forces. The *4e Régiment de Dragons* employed a new organization during the operation based on half of that being considered for the future Leclerc regiments, (which each consisted of two forty-tank *groupe d'escadrons*).

There were also equipment problems. The 4e RD's AMX-30B2s were not fully equipped with the DIVT-16 CASTOR thermal camera system, and they had to trade a proportion of their tanks with other units to make up this deficiency. The *2e Escadron* took a large number of CASTOR equipped tanks from the *1e Régiment de Cuirassiers*. The decision to send a full regiment of tanks was only taken very late in French planning. It was originally envisioned to only send one of the army's two professionalized armoured squadrons (the 1/4e RD or 2/501e RCC) to spearhead the *Daguet* operation. The French Army Chief of Staff intervened to allow a larger armoured unit to be included following the advice of the 6e DLB commander, *Général* Mouscardès.

The men of the *Division Daguet* saw combat during the advance into Kuwait, engaging dug-in T55 tanks of the Iraqi 45th Division without loss, and performing to expectation as the van of the 6e DLB (which also deployed the AMX-10RC and VAB

armoured personnel carrier). Saudi AMX-30S battle tanks and Qatari AMX-30Bs also saw combat defending the Saudi town of Khafji (and during the liberation of Kuwait), where they fought a two day armoured battle alongside US forces. The sands of the deserts of Kuwait and Iraq would be the AMX-30's only taste of combat in French service, and in contrast to modern tanks like the M1A1 Abrams and Challenger 1 the AMX-30B2's armour protection looked painfully inadequate. With GIAT's delivery of the Leclerc slipping repeatedly and the inadequate level of protection of the AMX-30B2, measures were finally taken to improve the type's poor armour protection in 1995.

Brennus

GIAT was contracted to develop an explosive reactive armour (ERA) system to be employed on the AMX-30B2 before 1991, but due to the détente in East-West relations the program was not given much urgency. Two demonstration vehicles based on early AMX-30B2 vehicles equipped with the DIVT-13 camera system were shown by GIAT in 1991, but the system was not ordered for several years. By the time of the reactive armour system's introduction it was only procured for a limited number of AMX-30B2 tanks of France's rapid reaction corps. Funding was the major roadblock to providing the entire AMX-30B2 fleet with the Brennus modifications, but with the Leclerc on the near horizon there was little point in converting a large number of AMX-30B2s.

The Brennus conversions would probably have never been undertaken at all had the situation in the Balkans after 1993 not spiralled completely out of control. The ability of the AMX-30B2 to resist infantry antitank weapons was inadequate in the event of an armed intervention in Yugoslavia by French forces under the NATO umbrella, and the Brennus program was a cheap and effective solution. The AMX-30B2 Brennus conversions were executed on about 90 AMX-30B2 tanks with hydrostatic cooling systems, tanks from the last conversion batches completed by the Roanne plant.

Rheinweiler 1743, **showing one of the FORAD tanks without the rear fuel drums, which are strictly fitted to change the vehicle silhouette.**
[Jonathan Cany]

Another rear layout on one of the FORAD tanks shows the retention of a single jerry can rack on the rear plate between the two fuel drums. [Thomas Seignon]

All AMX-30B2 Brennus tanks mounted the DIVT-16 Castor thermal gunnery camera. The most visible feature was 112 GIAT BS G2 explosive reactive armour bricks fitted to the hull glacis, and to the front and sides of the turret. These bricks weighed only some twelve kilograms each and incorporated a four hundred gram plastic explosive charge sandwiched between layers of hardened steel and kevlar. The system was alleged to give the same protection as 400mm armour steel for a weight gain of just over one tonne. The Brennus conversion was named for an ancient chief, the Gaul chieftain who assaulted the city of Rome some three hundred and fifty years before the Common Era.

The Brennus modifications concerned more than a simple armour package. The later modifications seen on the Brennus

The CENZUB center at Sissonne is home to a second FORAD element. Here we can see early experiments at an urban camouflage scheme being tested out on an AMX-30B2. By the end of the first decade of the new century a camouflage scheme reminiscent of the old British Berlin scheme was being tested out as a logical scheme for the CENZUB vehicles. [Thomas Seignon]

A CENZUB FORAD AMX-30B2 about to set out for a day of training in 2013. [Jonathan Cany]

vehicles (and shared with the artillery's modernized AuF-1 SPG) were added incrementally. The Gallix grenade launching system successfully tested on the AMX-30B2 in *Daguet* was installed to supplement the original four 81mm smoke dischargers as the second component of the Brennus' armour system. This was a system first seen on the AMX-40 and adopted for the Leclerc program. On the AMX-30B2 Brennus it incorporated a large sensor unit on the turret roof and two grenade launcher clusters. The AMX-30B2 Brennus was issued first to the amalgamated 501e-503e RCC and to the *2e Régiment de Chasseurs* in 1995.

The later modifications seen on the Brennus vehicles included the installation of a 750 horsepower Mack E-9 engine (which was employed together with the existing Minerva ENC-200 transmission without any major hull modifications) and new Diehl tracks. The new engine gave the type more power and better acceleration. These modifications were made after the Brennus tanks were grouped into the combined *1e-2e Régiment*

de Chasseurs in 1996. The amalgamations of the mid-1990s resulted in all of the Brennus tanks being concentrated into only one regiment.

A full regiment of AMX-30B2 Brennus tanks could have been deployed had the situation in the Balkans ever warranted it, but in the end these never actually left France. The Brennus was really intended as a stop-gap measure. The eighty tanks of the *1e-2e Régiment de Chasseurs* (which was an RC80 type regiment that eventually received the Leclerc) were based at Thierville sur Meuse. They received the upgraded tanks in 1996; operating them for some ten years. The larger war establishment of the *1e-2e Régiment de Chasseurs'* regimental organization was the same developed for the new Leclerc based on two 40 tank squadrons (or *groupes d'escadrons*). This order of battle was adopted in all regiments following thorough testing by the combined 4e RD and 501e RCC, concluded at Mourmelon in 1992 after the analysis of the *Daguet* deployment's lessons.

A spectacular series of shots taken in late 2013 show the FORAD AMX-30B2's during a range period. [Jonathan Cany]

Numbering perhaps 40 or 50 available AMX-30B2s, these are the last of the gun tanks in service, at the time of writing in 2014, some 47 years after entering service. [Jonathan Cany]

The AMX-30B2 remained in service in dwindling numbers thereafter, but ultimately with the arrival of the Leclerc finally assured and the Cold War over, the AMX-30B2 too was on borrowed time. When the Brennus vehicles were handed in for storage in 2006, the AMX-30 battle tank had already served as a front line battle tank for a remarkable 40 years. The AMX-30B2 Brennus was the ultimate gun tank version of the AMX-30 series and with a reliable powerpack and with improved protection, allied to what was still an adequate fire control system, it would no doubt have given a good account of itself had it ever seen combat.

The Brennus vehicles were stored, at first in war reserve and then for sale by Nexter (the national arms company that succeeded GIAT in 2004). As far as is known there were no interested parties and they eventually ended up on the target ranges (some 45 vehicles were for a time offered for sale by the Flanders Tech Supply company, though little information concerning the status of these vehicles is available). The AMX-30B2 continued in limited service even after the Brennus tanks were retired, mainly as training vehicles. Others sat in dumps as parts vehicles for the large number of derivatives in service. By 2000 a large proportion of the AMX-30 fleet was already retired. Between 2006 and 2009 some 356 additional AMX-30 series gun tanks were disposed of, leaving a handful in service.

The final chapter in the AMX-30 story is the AMX-30B2 FORAD (*Forces Adverses* or enemy forces) vehicles that fulfill the OPFOR role during major exercises. The FORAD was created from the *5e Régiment de Dragons*; itself the heir to one of the first AMX-30B equipped cavalry regiments, the old *30e Régiment de Dragons* of Valdahon (dissolved in 1978). At least two squadrons of FORAD tanks are kept operational, capable of participating in any manoeuvres in the Champagne area of eastern France. While many of the Mailly based tanks carry some cosmetic modifications to simulate a Soviet-built adversary they maintain fully functional main and co-axial armaments. They serve with other OPFOR vehicles suitably disguised as foreign AFVs to train Leclerc crews and mechanized infantry in realistic combat exercises. They cannot be considered as more than training vehicles, but even at the time of writing at the end of 2013, these FORAD AMX-30 tanks continue to serve at the *Centre d'Entrainement Au Combat* (CENTAC) at Mailly and at the *Centre de Combat en Zone Urbaine* (CENZUB) at Sissone.

The AMX-30 series of gun tanks were served by over four decades worth of young French conscripts and by long serving regulars. The 30-ton tanks are remembered fondly and with great pride by many who served in the *Arme Blindée Cavalerie*. The French Army, now a professional force with a different mis-

The muzzle flash of the 105mm CN F1 at the moment of firing. [Jonathan Cany]

Under cover of smoke, FORAD AMX-30B2s advancing during a public display. [Jonathan Cany]

The only combat that the AMX-30 gun tanks saw in French colours was in 1991, some 24 years into its long career. Here we can see an AMX-30B2 of the *4e Régiment de Dragons* on March 3rd 1991 at the end of *Operation Daguet*. The Gallix system is quite obvious despite the large amount of stowage on the turret. [United States Department of Defence, SSgt D. Wagner]

sion to that of the Cold War era conscript force, still maintains a bond to the light cavalry philosophy of warfare it adopted in the 1950s. The AMX-30B and derivatives were the first products of that philosophy. They have in their time provided their country a long and loyal service.

Bibliography

Fromion, Y. and Diebold, J. *Rapport d'Information Deposé par la Commission de la Défense Nationale et des Forces Armeés sur la Situation de GIAT Industries.* Rapport No.474 Assemblée Nationale. France 2002.

Les Industries d'Armement de l'État: Rapport au Président de la République Suivi des Réponses des Administrations et des Organismes Intéressées. Cour des Comptes. France October 2001

Palagos, J.-M., Ollivier, Y., Barthelemy, F., Laumonier, F., Barbet, D. Dudognon, J.-P. *Rapport du Groupe d'Enquête Interministériel sur l'Exportation des Materiels de Guerre en Fin de Vie.* France 29 May 2006

Jackson, P.J. (Major, United States Army) *French Ground Force Organizational Development for Counterrevolutionary Warfare Between 1945 and 1962.* Thesis, Faculty of the US Army Command and General Staff College. Fort Leavenworth Kansas 2005.

Jeudi, Jean-Gabriel. *Chars de France.* Editions ETAI, Paris 1999.

Ogorkiewicz, Richard. AFV Profile 63 *AMX-30 Battle Tank* Profile Publications, Windsor, U.K., 1977.

Marest, M. and Tauzin, M. *L'Armement de Gros Calibre. Comité Pour l'Histoire des Armements Terrestres Tome 9.* Centre des Hautes Études de l'Armement, Division Histoire. France 2008.

The works of Pierre Touzin and the late Yves Debay were also consulted throughout the researching of this book.

Technical Publications, Arme Blindée Cavalrie

AMX-30 Notice de Mise en Œuvre et d'Instruction No.256, (Chassis Figures) Saumur 1975.

Documentation Technique Edition de 1994 *AMX-30B2 (Chassis texte)* Saumur 1994.

Documentation Technique Edition de 1994 *AMX-30B2 (Chassis figures)* Saumur 1994.

ABC 101-11 Manuel d'Emploi de l'Escadron AMX-30B2. Edition de 1998 Ministère de la Defense. France, 1998.

Rear view of the AMX-30B2: the rear plate was different in layout from the earlier AMX-30B, with the infantry phone box moved to the center of the plate, and with the towing clevis relocated to the front of the hull. [Pierre Delattre]

The left front of the turret: 20mm Cn F2, PH-8B searchlight and the shape of the bottom of the mantlet casting of this AMX-30B2 conversion. We can also see the new gunnery sights on the turret roof and the new armoured jacket for the cupola machine gun. [Pierre Delattre]

The right side of the turret seen from the front three quarters, with the DIVT-13 Low Light Television Camera and the very obvious former location of the old rangefinder ears. This vehicle was converted from an AMX-30B, probably in the mid 1980s. [Pierre Delattre]

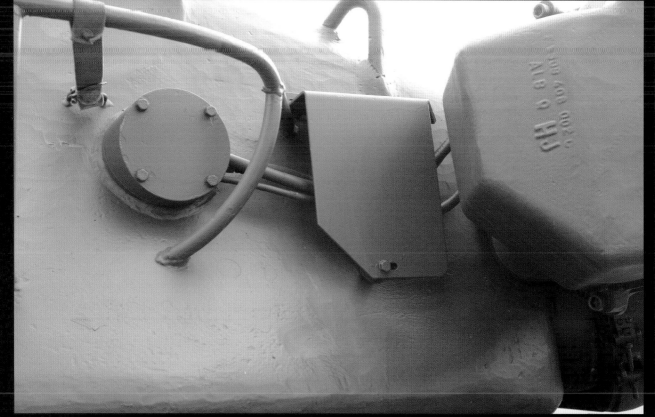

The wiring system for the DIVT-13. The DIVT-13 was an effective if vulnerable system for night combat. [Pierre Delattre]

The modified cupola machine gun mounting on top of the TOP7 cupola. [Pierre Delattre]

The old PH-8B searchlight endured for many years as a normal searchlight after its use as a night fighting system ceased. Here we can see the wiring for the PH-8B preserved on this mid series AMX-30B2. [Pierre Delattre]

The NBC system was relocated to the rear turret bin, which had a revised shape to accommodate the filtration system. The frame welded to the top of the NBC box was used to stow the PH-8B. [Pierre Delattre]

The vent for the crew compartment heater. [Pierre Delattre]

The engine deck of the AMX-30B2 was not vastly different from the AMX-30B, and employed the HS-110-2 engine, which was rated for a higher horsepower output. [Pierre Delattre]

The protection grills fitted over the mufflers and exhaust seen on the AMX-30B2 were frequently used on exercise as extemporised barbecues, and we also fitted to the later AMX-30Bs. [Pierre Delattre]

The towing clevis was relocated to the right front wing. [Pierre Delattre]

The right side of the AMX-30B2 turret [seen here in desert camouflage to represent an Operation Daguet vehicle]. We can see where the rangefinder ears were plated over and ground smooth. We can also see the track guards and dust plates fitted around the turret ring, normally available for desert operations. [Pierre Delattre]

The Thales DIVT-16 CASTOR thermal gunnery camera, and the layout of the ERA bricks on the mantlet, the front slope of the turret roof and on the turret sides are visible. [Pierre Delattre]

The glacis plate and mantlet seen from the lower angle on an AMX-30B2 Brennus. The rightside driver's periscope was extended to allow a clear view over the bulky ERA array. [Pierre Delattre]

The Gallix system, pioneered on the AMX-30B2s deployed in Operation Daguet in 1991, and adopted as standard on the Brennus. Here we see the smoke grenade launchers. [Pierre Delattre]

The ERA side arrays on the AMX-30B2 Brennus. Notice the stowage of old tracklinks despite the vehicle's new Diehl tracks. [Pierre Delattre]

The rear stowage baskets fitted to compensate for the bulk of the new armour system. [Pierre Delattre]

The stowage previously carried in the rear stowage bin was moved to the left side of the NBC box on the AMX-30B2, which was carried forward to the Brennus. We can also see the late pattern tactical markings. [Pierre Delattre]

The left side of the turret, showing the main sensor system for the Galix system on the left side of the turret roof, the smoke dischargers and the ERA array. [Pierre Delattre]

The Brennus' ERA system was mounted on brackets that held the individual reactive armour bricks away from the armour of the turret and hull. [Pierre Delattre]

The cluttered turret and hull of the Brennus. [Pierre Delattre]

The front view of the DIVT-16 thermal gunnery camera system mounted on the AMX-30B2 Brennus. [Pierre Delattre]

Closeup of the right side of the mantlet. The main telescopic sight's location prevented a more complete protection for the gun mantlet. [Pierre Delattre]

Left side of the gun mantlet, we can see some of the brackets behind the ERA bricks. [Pierre Delattre]

Augueld 1805 **seen from the left side.** **[Pierre Delattre]**

Side view of the DIVT-16 system camera barbette, which was hinged outward to permit access and maintenance. [Pierre Delattre]

The turret bustle of the AMX-30B2 Brennus is barely visible behind the clutter of stowage boxes and stowage baskets. Note how the original smoke dischargers were retained. [Pierre Delattre]

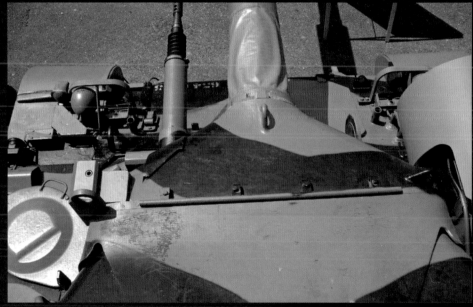

Top view of the mantlet joint cover and mantlet of a FORAD AMX-30B2. [Zurich 2RD]

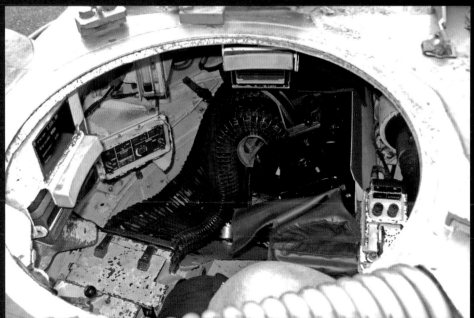

View through the Romeo-Charlie's open hatch, the loader's position is visible along with the feed system for the 20mm Cn F2. [Zurich 2RD]

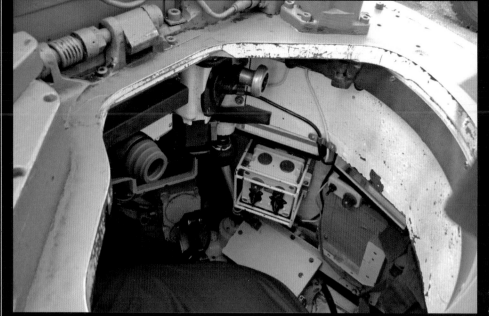

View through the Commander's open hatch. [Zurich 2RD]

The bottom of a disguised DIVT-16 CASTOR system on a FORAD AMX-30B2 [Zurich 2RD]

The open gun sight cover, employed to seal and protect the main gunner's telescope in the gun mantlet. [Zurich 2RD]

The driver's position. [Zurich 2RD]

The driver's position seen from inside the turret where the loader/radio operator sits. [Zurich 2RD]

The gunner's position in the AMX-30B2. [Zurich 2RD]

One of the old war horses of the CENZUB FORAD during Exercise *Azur* in 2006. **[Pierre Delattre]**

The Cn 105 F1 gun's breech. The AMX-30B2 employed an internal gun crutch, seen in the engaged position here. [Zurich 2RD]

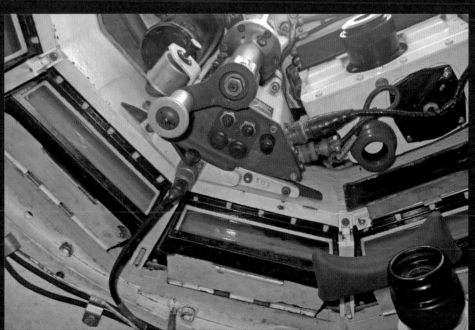

The TOP7 cupola seen from the inside looking up. [Zurich 2RD]

The front slope of the AMX-30B2 Brennus, filthy with Champagne chalk and cluttered with ERA bricks. [Zurich 2RD]

The AMX-30B2 Brennus' turret bustle NBC box with the stowage basket fitted. The Brennus did not employ the old PH-8B searchlight, and its stowage location was replaced with this stowage basket. [Zurich 2RD]

The AMX-30B2 Brennus turret trained to the 2 o'clock postion, we can see the arrangement of the ERA bricks, and the 20mm Cn F2 co-axial armament. [Pierre Delattre]

The uneven placement of the ERA bricks on the AMX-30B2 Brennus's turret front roof slope, at the bottom center we can just see the location for the old PH-8B mounting. [Pierre Delattre]

Loader's periscope, Galix sensor, and the Galix system's 6 barrelled smoke/flare dischargers. [Pierre Delattre]

The Mack E9 motor used on the AMX-30B2 Brennus in its final configuration led to some further changes on the engine deck layout. The frontal armour suite meant that the battery covers were mounted on the engine deck. [Pierre Delattre]

The AMX-30B2 Brennus' turret roof, seen here is the area around the loader's hatch. [Pierre Delattre]

Another view of the Brennus' engine deck. [Pierre Delattre]

The rear of the Galix system. It is a stoutly built unit also carried by the Leclerc, albeit in a far more discreet form. [Pierre Delattre]

The armoured cupola machine gun box carried by the AMX-30B2 [in this case on an AMX-30B2 Brennus] in the open position. [Pierre Delattre]

The side stowage box on the front left side of the hull in the open position. [Pierre Delattre]

The DX-175 simulator system fitted to this tank was widely used as a training aid in the French Army in the 1990s and to this day. The 20mm Cn F2 is not mounted. [Pierre Delattre]

This AMX-30B2 wearing *5e Régiment de Cuirassiers* insignia is a late AMX-30B2 conversion, based on a rebuilt AMX-30B but carrying the DIVT-16 thermal camera seen fitted to AMX-30B2 conversions from 1988-1989 onwards. [Pierre Delattre]

The fire simulator for the DX-175 fitted to the front of the AMX-30B2's turret. [Pierre Delattre]

Here we can see the very tight clearance for the AMX-30's driver on an AMX-30B2 of the CENZUB FORAD during Exercise Azur in 2006. [Pierre Delattre]

The DX175 fit includes a combined amber flasher and sensor unit that bolts to the basket rails on each side of the turret. [Pierre Delattre]

The DIVT-16 CASTOR system. We can also see the late style SNCF markings, the army emblem on the plated-over rangefinder holes and the sunken appearance of these plates. The new-build AMX-30B2s of the 1982-1984 batches used new cast turrets without these tell tale depressions, but they were a rarity by the early 2000s because they did not receive the DIVT-16. [Pierre Delattre]

Rear view of the *Augueld 1805*. [**Pierre Delattre**]

The vast vehicle park at Draguignan held this sad collection of AMX-30Bs and AMX-30B2s in 2006. These vehicles serve as a vast but finite source of spare parts. [Pierre Delattre]

Long serving, and worked hard, the AMX-30B2 will probably serve for a few years yet in the FORAD role. [Pierre Delattre]

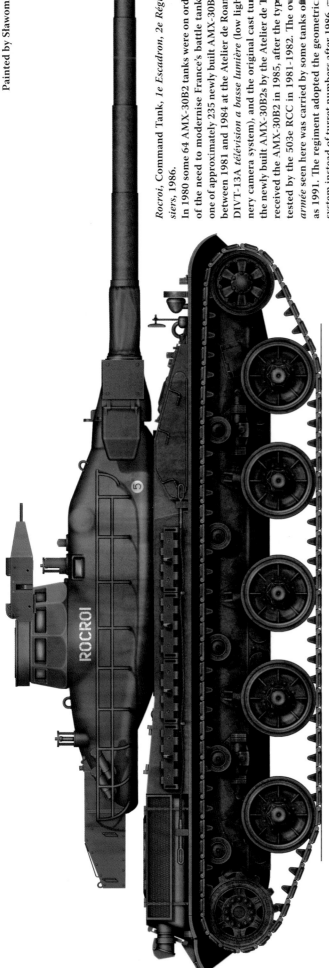

Rocroi, Command Tank, *1e Escadron, 2e Régiment de Cuirassiers*, 1986.

In 1980 some 64 AMX-30B2 tanks were on order in recognition of the need to modernise France's battle tank. The *Rocroi* was one of approximately 235 newly built AMX-30B2 tanks produced between 1981 and 1984 at the Atelier de Roanne. It carries the DIVT-13A *télévision a basse lumière* (low light television gunnery camera system), and the original cast turret produced for the newly built AMX-30B2s by the Atelier de Tarbes. The 2e RC received the AMX-30B2 in 1985, after the type was thoroughly tested by the 503e RCC in 1981-1982. The overall coat of *vert armée* seen here was carried by some tanks of the 2e RC as late as 1991. The regiment adopted the geometric tactical marking system instead of turret numbers after 1986, and *Rocroi* carried a grey square and X on the turret rear box a the *1e Escadron* command tank.

AMX-30E, unknown regiment, Spanish Army, 1990s.

Spain was granted a production license to build the AMX-30E in 1973 after having bought a small batch of 19 AMX-30B tanks in 1970. Nearly 300 production AMX-30E gun tanks were assembled from French and Spanish components starting in 1974 at the Santa Barbara plant. The Spanish AMX-30 experience was not an entirely positive one because of the AMX transmission's fragility. In the middle of the 1980s 140 tanks received a new Allison transmission (AMX-30EM2). A further improvement program (AMX-30EM1) adopted for the remaining 150 tanks included a laser rangefinder, new MTU engine and new transmission. The rebuilt AMX-30E series were retired in the late 1990s and early 2000s in favour of the Leopard 2A4 MBT and the *Centauro* heavy armoured car.

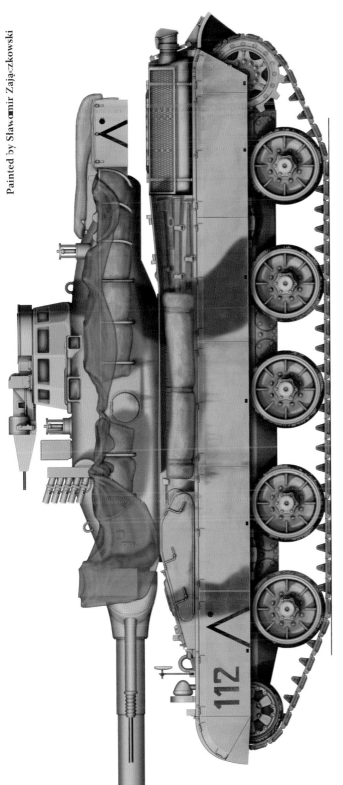

112

AMX-30B2 *4e Régiment de Dragons, Operation Daguet,*
February 1991.

The AMX-30B2 was France's heaviest armour option available to equip the spearhead of the *6e Division Légère Blindée* for action against the Iraqi forces occupying Kuwait. The use of large tactical numbers (usually applied on the sand shields) on most of the regiment's tanks was readopted for the operation. The 4e RD's AMX-30B2s carried the coalition chevron marking on the sand shields, engine decks, PH-8 searchlight doors, and rear NBC box, apparently to no set pattern. The regiment was manned by professionals drawn from across the *Arme Blindée Cavalerie* to make up the necessary numbers for *Daguet.*

AMX-30B2 Brennus, 1e-2e Regiment de Chasseurs, France,
1997.

The Brennus was the ultimate development of the AMX-30B2 gun tank introduced in 1995-1996. The 80 Brennus tanks that equipped the 1e-2e RCh were modernized in 1997 with the Mack E9 engine and new tracks common to the modernized AuF-1. Turret markings for the 1e-2e RCh AMX-30B2 Brennus were sparse because of the ERA arrays: vehicle names were usually painted on the right side of the gun barrel, and simple low-visibility grey geometric tactical symbols were carried on the rear of the NBC box. The *immatriculation,* NATO tactical symbol and bridging discs were seen on the front and rear of the vehicle in the standard locations.

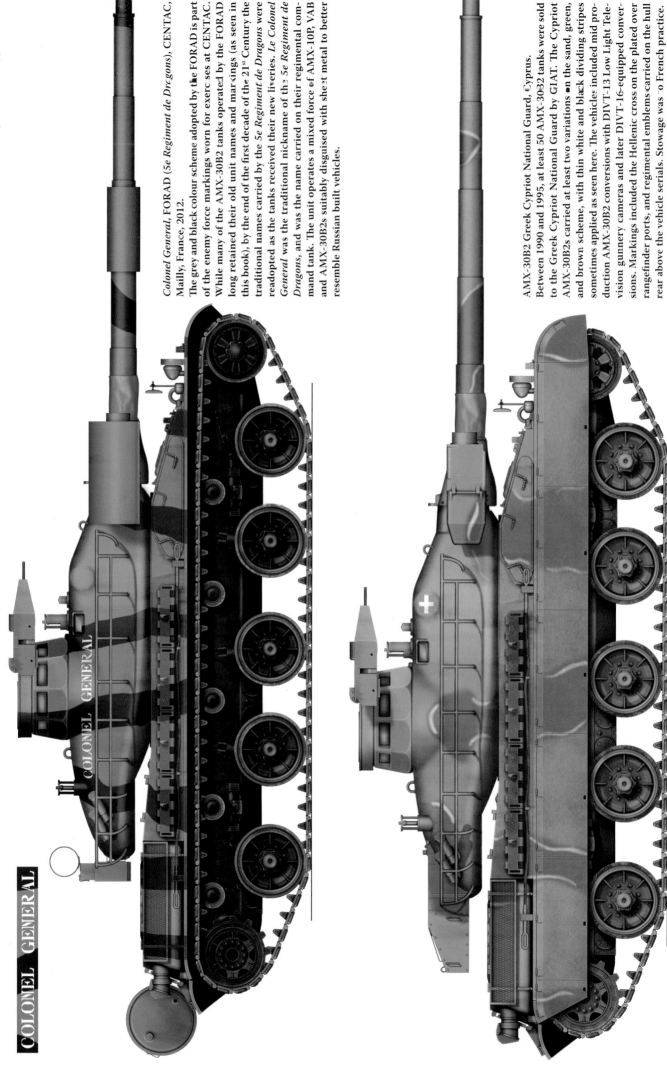

Painted by Sławomir Zajączkowski

COLONEL GENERAL

Colonel General, FORAD (*5e Regiment de Dragons*), CENTAC, Mailly, France, 2012.

The grey and black colour scheme adopted by the FORAD is part of the enemy force markings worn for exercises at CENTAC. While many of the AMX-30B2 tanks operated by the FORAD long retained their old unit names and markings (as seen in this book), by the end of the first decade of the 21st Century the traditional names carried by the *5e Regiment de Dragons* were readopted as the tanks received their new liveries. *Le Colonel General* was the traditional nickname of the *5e Regiment de Dragons*, and was the name carried on their regimental command tank. The unit operates a mixed force of AMX-10P, VAB and AMX-30B2s suitably disguised with sheet metal to better resemble Russian built vehicles.

AMX-30B2 Greek Cypriot National Guard, Cyprus.

Between 1990 and 1995, at least 50 AMX-30B2 tanks were sold to the Greek Cypriot National Guard by GIAT. The Cypriot AMX-30B2s carried at least two variations on the sand, green, and brown scheme, with thin white and black dividing stripes sometimes applied as seen here. The vehicles included mid production AMX-30B2 conversions with DIVT-13 Low Light Television gunnery cameras and later DIVT-16-equipped conversions. Markings included the Hellenic cross on the plated over rangefinder ports, and regimental emblems carried on the hull rear above the vehicle serials. Stowage was to French practice.

KAGERO.EU

READ FOR FREE
on KAGERO's Area

LIST OF PUBLICATION SERIES

TopColors

miniTopColors

Units

TopDrawings

  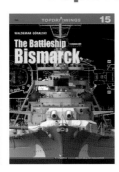  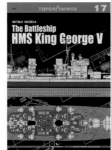 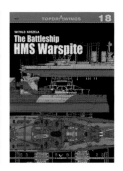

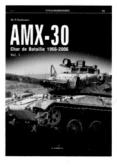
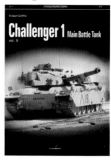

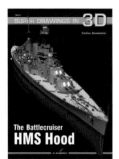
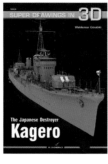
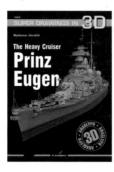
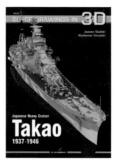

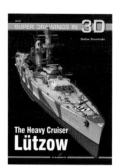